More Praise for *Overcoming*

"I found *Overcoming Anxiety* to be an exceptionally reader/user-friendly resource and workbook. It is easy to understand, interesting, and comprehensively informative."

—Bonnie Goodman, M.S., L.M.H.C.,
coauthor of *You Have Choices:
Recovering from Anxiety, Panic, and
Phobia*

"A reading must for all those who suffer from the devastation of anxiety and panic-related disorders."

—Marilyn Gellis, Ph.D., author of
*The Twelve Steps of Phobics
Anonymous*

"Long-time anxiety and panic sufferers take heart. Here is a hands-on, step-by-step strategy for attaining the deep-level change you need to make a recovery from persistent anxiety and panic."

—Sandra Festian, A.C.S.W., Iron
Mountain, Michigan

"Mr. Peurifoy's excellent balance of looking at all the areas of one's life is invaluable for people who have previously only had unidimensional approaches to treatment."

—Barbara E. Thompson, M.A.;
marriage, family and child
therapist; certified group
therapist; and executive director
of the Discovery Center

Overcoming Anxiety

Overcoming Anxiety

From Short-Term Fixes to
Long-Term Recovery

Reneau Z. Peurifoy,
M.A., M.F.C.C.

An Owl Book
Henry Holt and Company   New York

Henry Holt and Company, Inc.
Publishers since 1866
115 West 18th Street
New York, New York 10011

Henry Holt® is a registered
trademark of Henry Holt and Company, Inc.

Published in Canada by Fitzhenry & Whiteside Ltd.,
195 Allstate Parkway, Markham, Ontario L3R 4T8.

Library of Congress Cataloging-in-Publication Data
Peurifoy, Reneau Z.
Overcoming anxiety: from short-term fixes to long-term recovery /
Reneau Z. Peurifoy—1st ed.
p.   cm.
"An Owl book."
Includes bibliographical references and index.
1. Anxiety—Popular works.   I. Title.
RC531.P43 1997   96-29376
616.85′223—dc20   CIP

ISBN 0-8050-4789-1

Henry Holt books are available for special
promotions and premiums. For details contact:
Director, Special Markets.

First Owl Book Edition—1997

DESIGNED BY PAULA R. SZAFRANSKI

Printed in the United States of America
All first editions are printed on acid-free paper. ∞

1   3   5   7   9   10   8   6   4   2

Contents

Preface xv

Acknowledgments xvii

Chapter 1:
A New Way of Looking at Anxiety 1

What Is Long-Term Recovery? 3
How to Get the Most out of This Program 6
Summary of Key Ideas 7
Recommended Activities 8

Chapter 2: The Imprint of Childhood 15

Mary 16
Robert 21
Kimberly 25
Summary of Key Ideas 29
Recommended Activities 29

Contents

Chapter 3: The Time Tunnel   31

Conditioned Responses   32
Posttraumatic Stress Disorder   32
The Time Tunnel   35
Escaping the Time Tunnel   36
Four Common Traits in Adults with
    Abusive Childhoods   37
Summary of Key Ideas   40
Recommended Activities   40

Chapter 4: The Mystery of Emotions   47

What Are Emotions?   48
Why Do We Have Emotions?   49
Human Needs   52
Core Beliefs and Unconscious Associations   55
Summary of Key Ideas   57
Recommended Activities   58

**Chapter 5:
Developing Your Explanation for "Why"**   64

The Answer Is *E*   67
Five Factors That Can Trigger Symptoms   70
Mary's, Robert's, and Kimberly's
    Simple Explanations   75
Summary of Key Ideas   79
Recommended Activities   80

Chapter 6: Basic Symptom-Management Skills   87

Cue-Controlled Relaxation Response   88
Relaxed Diaphragmatic Breathing   89
Coping Self-Statements   91

Contents

Externalization/Distraction   96
Summary of Key Ideas   98
Recommended Activities   99

Chapter 7: Distorted Thinking   103

Distorted Thinking   104
Overgeneralizations   104
Magnification/Minimization   108
Emotional Reasoning   109
Challenging Irrational and Negative Self-Talk   112
Summary of Key Ideas   115
Recommended Activities   116

Chapter 8: Progressive Desensitization   120

Developing a Plan   120
Basic Guidelines for Practicing   124
Examples   127
Four-Step Approach to "What Ifs"   130
Increased Suggestibility   133
Summary of Key Ideas   135
Recommended Activities   136

Chapter 9:
Moving from Basic to Advanced Symptom Control   139

Achieving Basic Symptom Control   139
First Steps to Advanced Symptom Control   141
Confronting Death and Uncertainty   145
Shame   148
Summary of Key Ideas   149
Recommended Activities   150

Contents

Chapter 10: Establishing Healthy Boundaries   153

What Are Boundaries in Human Relationships?   154
Missing Anxiety's Message   155
What Should I Do?   157
Honoring Your Rights   160
The Excessive Need for Approval   161
Summary Sheets   162
Summary of Key Ideas   165
Recommended Activities   166

Chapter 11:
Detours along the Path to Recovery   170

Practice, Practice, Practice   171
Relearning Is Easier Than Starting from Scratch   175
More Bumps along the Road to
   Long-Term Recovery   180
D.E.R. Scripts   181
Honoring Your Responsibility to Respect the
   Rights of Others   184
Summary of Key Ideas   186
Recommended Activities   187

Chapter 12: Two Important "Quiet" Messages   189

Quiet Message One: Learn to Manage Periods
   of High Stress   189
Quiet Message Two: Find a Source of
   Spiritual Strength   192
Developing a Message Checklist   194
Summary of Key Ideas   196
Recommended Activities   197

Contents

Chapter 13: Viewing Yourself in a New Way   201

Your Self-Image   201
What Makes Me Valuable?   205
Perfectionism   209
Mistakes Are Terrible   211
Learning to Become Friends with Your Emotions   213
Unexpected Anger   214
Learning to "Normalize" Yourself   215
Summary of Key Ideas   217
Recommended Activities   218

Chapter 14: Final Steps   219

Where Do I Go from Here?   221
What If I'm Feeling Stuck?   221
Applying Your Skills to Other Areas of Your Life   222
A Final Word   224

**Appendix 1: The Main Types of
 Anxiety Disorders**   226

**Appendix 2: Guidelines for Selecting
 a Therapist**   233

Appendix 3: How to Locate Support Groups   239

**Appendix 4: How to Develop a
 Relaxation Response**   242

Supplemental Materials   246

Recommended Reading   248

Index   255

Preface

In 1988, I completed work on my first book, *Anxiety, Phobias, and Panic: Taking Charge and Conquering Fear,* and became the first person to present an integrated, "multimodal" treatment approach at a national conference on anxiety. In the years that followed, this approach became the standard course of treatment for people working with anxiety, and *Anxiety, Phobias, and Panic* became the book of choice among individuals, treatment facilities, therapists, and self-help groups working with anxiety both in the United States and in Europe.

As I completed revisions for the updated second edition of *Anxiety, Phobias, and Panic* in 1992, I knew that, as good as it was, something more was needed. In conversations with therapists and leaders of self-help groups nationwide, I became increasingly aware that while the treatment models being used were providing relief from anxiety, they were not enough. Like many other therapists, I was focusing more and more in my own practice on helping clients move beyond the initial stages of symptom control to what I now call long-term recovery.

PREFACE

As a result, I began working on this book in 1993 with the goal that it would move beyond my first work, break new ground, and show people suffering from anxiety how to achieve long-term recovery. After completing an outline and four chapters, I had to delay work on the initial draft for a year and a half to work on another project. This delay helped me develop the ideas that had been roughed out with numerous clients and has made the final work much more mature.

Because this book focuses on achieving long-term recovery and the "messages" behind anxiety, it presents the "basics" of symptom control in a simplified manner. Readers who want a more detailed explanation of this aspect of managing anxiety will find it useful to refer to my first book, *Anxiety, Phobias, and Panic*.

It is my hope that the struggles and victories of the people described in this book will help you live a fuller and more satisfying life. If you take the time to follow their example, I sincerely believe that you will succeed in your struggle with anxiety and achieve long-term recovery.

Acknowledgments

This book would have been impossible if not for the hundreds of people who shared their lives with me. Thank you for the insights you have given me and the help that my work with you will provide the readers of this book.

I would like to thank Laura DaLanni, Sandra Festian, Nancy Flocchini, Jane Hoff, John Marzo, Lynn Maguire, Debbie Roth, and Kay Stathacopoulos, who read the original draft and gave many suggestions for additions and changes. Alissyn Link went through the second draft and helped shape it into its final form.

Others I would like to thank include Rita Clark, who recommended two of the above readers, and Shirley Green, who has been a great source of encouragement over the years. In addition, Barbara-J. Zitwer, my agent, believed in my work during the early years when I was struggling to get it out to the public and has also been a tremendous source of encouragement. At Henry Holt, my copy editor, Jenna Dolan, did an outstanding job. Through her meticulous work, she caught numerous errors and greatly

ACKNOWLEDGMENTS

improved many sections of the book. Brian Oettel, then Amy Rosenthal were the editors who oversaw the project.

I would also like to thank my wife, Michiyo, who has patiently stood by my side while I've gained the experience and knowledge necessary to write this book.

Finally, I would like to thank my parents. Without them I would not be who I am today. I dedicate this book to them.

Overcoming Anxiety

1

A New Way of Looking at Anxiety

Since I first began working with anxiety-related problems in 1981, there has been an explosion of knowledge in the causes of and treatments for them. Today there's a flood of books and audio and video cassettes that describe programs for overcoming anxiety-related problems, as well as an increasing number of centers and therapists who specialize in treating them. Amid all this good news there is a sour note that is often not heard: Research has shown that the approaches currently being used to treat anxiety-related problems do work and provide relief, but they often fail as long-term solutions.

A tremendous number of people with anxiety-related problems go to a specialist or work through a self-help program and experience good results. However, after a period of time that can range from a few weeks to many years, the symptoms return. For some, the symptoms return in full force with debilitating anxiety and panic attacks and the redevelopment of avoidance behaviors or rituals. For others, the symptoms return at a level that is lower than originally experienced, or take a somewhat different form, which might include excessive worry or nervousness. It might also include avoidance behavior or nervous rituals that are different from those that accompanied the original onset of severe anxiety.

There are also many people who go through programs or read books and never find the relief they are seeking. Their initial intense symptoms may be greatly reduced, but they continue to experience a significant level of anxiety-related symptoms in spite of treatment. When anxiety symptoms return, or are never fully resolved, the sense of failure, anger, confusion, and depression that occurs can be overwhelming.

This book takes the next step in the evolution of solutions for anxiety and shows you how to move beyond what have been found to be short-term fixes to achieve long-term recovery. As you work your way through the chapters, you'll meet three people who have taken this next step, battled the crippling effects of severe anxiety, and won. Their battle was not an easy one nor was it over quickly. However, all three did eventually achieve long-term recovery. As you read about how they accomplished this, you will learn many new things about yourself, gain many new skills, and develop a new way of looking at anxiety.

One of the central themes of this book is that anxiety is simply a "messenger" that is telling you that you have one or more important life issues to address. Sometimes symptoms develop because a person is overwhelmed by too many things going on at the same time, such as problems with health, money, children, or work. However, anxiety can also be connected with problems in relationships (your ability to connect and be intimate with others) as well as with what are often called "existential" issues (how we answer the questions "What is the meaning of life?" and "How do I find happiness?").

The purpose of this book is to help you understand the message your symptoms are sending you. All too often, it is easy to become so focused on the symptoms of anxiety (the messenger) that you fail to understand the message. Learning to identify the message lifts the feeling of shame and demoralization that develops when you're focused on the elimination of symptoms. It's also the key to achieving what I call long-term recovery.

Once this idea is accepted, the goal shifts from the *absence* of anxiety to the *management* of anxiety. This is a more reasonable goal. Once the focus becomes the message (the underlying issues generating the anxiety) rather than the messenger (the symptoms), long-term recovery is possible.

What Is Long-Term Recovery?

Long-term recovery is really the final stage of the *process* that people recovering from anxiety go through. As people move through this process, they achieve progressively higher levels of recovery. For the sake of simplicity, I've divided these into the following three basic levels:

Level One: Basic Symptom Control

At this stage of recovery a person is focused on controlling symptoms. Indeed, this is always my initial focus with new clients. When they're experiencing intense symptoms, people simply aren't interested in long-term answers. They want relief and they want it *now!*

By the end of this stage, however, a person has made much improvement. Anxiety symptoms are greatly reduced with only occasional episodes of intense anxiety or panic, and there is usually the ability to function comfortably in at least half of the everyday situations that were formerly uncomfortable.

A person at the end of this stage also has a good understanding of the mechanisms of anxiety, along with a broad range of coping skills for managing symptoms. While no longer *hyper*vigilant (always on guard, watching for symptoms), this person is still moderately on guard. For many, medication continues to play a major role in symptom management.

Level Two: Advanced Symptom Control

A person in this stage of recovery is gaining greater confidence in his skills due to the absence of most, if not all, avoidance behavior. Intense episodes of anxiety are now infrequent. To at least a moderate degree, he has come to terms with those aspects of his personality that can cause problems and, when present, the genetic predisposition that makes him prone to anxiety. He has gotten to the point where he will not let symptoms interfere with his behavior. He knows how to avoid the anxiety-panic cycle and use his various skills effectively. There is some understanding that symptoms are messengers.

A person at this stage who relied heavily on medication while at level one is now no longer using medication, using it at a reduced level, or reserving its use for situations that are especially anxiety provoking.

Although anxiety is still a fearful thing, there is now more awareness of the issues that trigger anxiety. The focus has shifted, at least in part, away from the symptoms to the causes of anxiety. However, because this understanding is incomplete, periodic flare-ups of moderate to intense symptoms still mysteriously occur. When this happens there is a tendency to move back to level one and again become preoccupied with symptoms and develop avoidance behaviors.

Level Three: Long-Term Recovery

A person at this level perceives anxiety in a completely different way from a person at the first two levels. Anxiety is seen as a natural part of life rather than as something to be avoided. A person at this level can easily identify her core issues and understand clearly and fully the various messages anxiety sends. When anxiety is experienced, she realizes that high levels of anxiety are *supposed* to occur when real-life issues are present, so she focuses on the issues generating her anxiety rather than on the symptoms. This, in turn, allows her to experience high levels of anxiety without the distress or escalating symptoms she experienced when her anxiety-related problems began. A person at this stage who formerly relied on medication for symptom control finds it is no longer needed.

Before proceeding, take a moment to decide which of the above levels best describes you at the moment. If this is the first book you've read on anxiety, you may still be caught in the initial intense symptoms and have yet to experience any relief. If you've been battling anxiety for years, you've probably read many books, been through one or more programs, or seen several therapists in your quest for recovery. In this case, you may have cycled back and forth between levels one and two. In either case, my goal is to give you the tools and the knowledge you need to achieve long-term recovery.

How to Get the Most out of This Program

This book is designed to be used as a *workbook*. In order to get the most out of it, you need to read through it slowly; I suggest you spend at least one week on each chapter and do as many of the recommended activities as possible. While it's best to work through the book systematically, some people just can't wait to learn what each chapter contains. If you are one of these, go ahead and read through the entire book to get a general idea of what it covers. Once you've done this, read the book all the way through, slowly.

In order to achieve the long-term recovery described in this chapter, you need more than just a general understanding of ideas. Your goal is to internalize the information and skills presented in each chapter, to make them a natural and automatic part of your behavior. The recommended activities play a key role in this process. The more time and energy you spend on them, the more successful you will be.

Beginning with the next chapter, plan to spend at least one week on each chapter before you move on to the next one. Start by reading the headings to get an overview of the material. Then read the whole chapter at your usual reading rate. It is best to read each chapter at least three times, more if you find the information difficult. The second and third readings will increase your understanding of the material and reveal ideas that were missed during the first reading.

There may be times when you could spend more than one week on a chapter. While it is important to be thorough, it is also important to maintain your momentum. Therefore, spend no more than two weeks on a chapter, and do as many of the recommended activities as possible. After completing the program, you can spend additional time on those areas where you feel more work is needed. This may sound like a lot of work; it is. But keep in mind that it took you all your life to develop the behaviors and thinking patterns that produced your condition. It will take you time, energy, and a strong commitment to learn new and effective ways of thinking and acting. If you work through the material in the manner outlined, chances are excellent that you will succeed.

Summary of Key Ideas

1. Anxiety is a normal part of life. It is a "messenger" that indicates the presence of a problem or issue that needs to be resolved. The more intense the anxiety, the more important the issue. People with severe anxiety often have important life issues they are not dealing with effectively.
2. Long-term recovery focuses on the *management* of anxiety rather than on the *absence* of anxiety.
3. There are three different levels of recovery possible. Many people become stuck at the first or second level, or cycle back and forth between the first two levels.
4. People who achieve long-term recovery perceive anxiety differently from those at the first two levels of recovery. When anxiety occurs, they understand the message and respond to it in an effective way. Because of this, they can experience high levels of anxiety without the distress or escalating symptoms they experienced when their anxiety-related problems began.
5. In order to achieve long-term recovery, you need to work through the program presented in this book in a slow and systematic manner.

Recommended Activities

Getting the Most out of the
Recommended Activities

At the end of each chapter is a set of activities many people have found valuable in achieving long-term recovery. You may find that some of the activities involve information or skills that are already a part of how you usually think and act. Or you may find that the material seems awkward, uncomfortable, or difficult. This is to be expected since this program is designed to meet the needs of many people and you are unique, with your own personal requirements and abilities. Spend less time with activities you find easy and more time with those that seem difficult.

The easy activities probably involve skills you have already practiced and ideas you have already internalized. The difficult ones probably involve skills and ideas that are new to you or that you've never really mastered. These are the ones that are the most important for you. However, if a particular activity causes undue stress or anxiety, it means you are not ready for it. Skip it and work on exercises that are less difficult. Then return to the stressful exercise later. You may find that it is not as stressful as when you first tried it.

One of the keys to achieving long-term recovery is developing the ability to hear the message that your symptoms are sending. Often this can be difficult. So, even though a particular exercise may not seem like it applies to you, do it anyway. You may be surprised by the results.

No one can say exactly how long it will take you to achieve long-term recovery. It depends on the genetic makeup of your body, your personality, and the complexity and difficulty of the issues from both your childhood and your present circumstances. It should also be noted that when you do achieve long-term recovery, you probably won't know it until you've been there for quite some time. This is the way personal growth takes place. However, if you have a strong commitment to use the book as it is designed—to do the reading and apply as many of the suggestions to your life as possible (even though you may think they are silly or may not fully understand why they are suggested)—it is very likely you will succeed.

Establish a Regular Study Time

As you work through this book, keep in mind that it is a *self-directed study program*. Establish a regular time to work with the activities at the end of the chapters, and make this scheduled study time as important as your regular meals. If you use a calendar or appointment book, record your study times in it. Having a regular study time helps you avoid the common mistake of working only when you are experiencing high levels of anxiety. Remember the "good day rule": *You can make the most progress when you are feeling good and your life seems to be running smoothly.* It is during these times that it is easiest to look at yourself objectively and do the activities listed in the chapters. It is also when you are least motivated to do them. Do them anyway. It is during your good days that you will be most able to develop the skills and understanding you need to achieve long-term recovery.

Write a Brief Explanation of Your Condition

Before you go on to the next chapter, write a brief explanation of why you think your symptoms developed and why they continue to be a problem. This explanation can range from one paragraph to a page in length. Keep this explanation so you can refer to it later.

Consider Using Supplemental Materials

This book can be used by itself, however, you may find supplemental materials helpful, especially if you are having trouble understanding or sticking with the written material. Helpful materials are described in the "Supplemental Materials" section at the end of the book.

Consider Psychotherapy

Although many people have used the approach in this book to achieve long-term recovery without the help of a psychotherapist, others have found it best to use it in conjunction with professional psychotherapy. If you are experiencing extreme difficulty coping with life, find a therapist experienced in working with anxiety-related problems. Guidelines on how to select a therapist are given in appendix 2.

Find a Study Partner

Although it is possible to work through this book on your own, many find it helpful to have a friend or relative read and work through the material with them. Your study partner does not need to be a person with anxiety-related problems, but he or she does need to be someone you trust and with whom you are comfortable. Discussing the chapters with a study partner deepens your understanding. This partner will also be able to help you discover things in the material you may not see on your own.

Consider Joining a Self-Help Group

Many people find that a self-help group is tremendously useful in helping them to achieve long-term recovery. A well-run support group offers the advantages of a study partner multiplied by the number of people in the group. Appendix 3 describes how to find a local self-help group.

A Word about Medication

Most clients come to therapy seeking a quick and easy solution that will return them to where they were before their distressing symptoms began. This is a normal reaction and explains the heavy reliance on medication so common among anxiety sufferers. In response to this demand, a wide variety of medications has been developed that can reduce anxiety symptoms. While they can be very useful in stabilizing a person who is feeling out of control, they are usually not a long-term solution. About half the people I see are put on medication prior to coming to me. The other half either have taken no medication or are using medication "as needed." Of the three case studies in this book, Mary was taking a tranquilizer as needed, Robert was on a regular dose of medication, and Kimberly had taken medication but did not like the side effects and had discontinued using it.

In each case I told them what I usually tell my clients: If you're taking medication, continue taking it as it has been prescribed.

Most of my clients do not like being on medication, but it is important to stay on any prescribed medication until you feel you've mastered the basic skills and are ready to begin reducing the dosage. When you feel you wish to go off your medication, be sure to consult the physician who prescribed it, and go off it gradually. If you've been taking medication regularly, *the sudden withdrawal from it may cause an increase in your symptoms or produce other adverse effects.*

If you are not taking medication and are able to function adequately, I encourage you to see what you can accomplish through the skills taught in this book. If your symptoms are making it difficult for you to function, then medication may help to reduce those symptoms enough so that you can cope with life while you work through this book. If you decide to try medication, I would recommend that you see a psychiatrist rather than a family physician. Psychiatrists specialize in psychoactive medications (medications that affect emotions and mental processes) and are better able to mix and adjust those medications when side effects occur. As with all physicians, seek a psychiatrist who listens carefully to you. The guidelines for selecting a therapist listed in appendix 2 also apply to psychiatrists.

One key exception to the above general guidelines is obsessive-compulsive disorder. Since this condition has a large biological component, medication is often helpful when used *in conjunction with* a cognitive behavioral approach, such as the one described in this book.

A Word to the Spouse or Significant Other of a Person with Anxiety-Related Problems

I strongly recommend that the spouse or significant other of a person with anxiety-related problems become educated about what his or her loved one is experiencing. Unfortunately, the spouse or significant other is often very fearful about or scornful toward his or her loved one's anxiety-related problems. Sometimes this is due to a secret fear that if the loved one gets better and becomes more independent, the relationship will end. Other times, it is because the spouse or significant other is dealing with issues that are similar to those of the loved one. Sometimes simple ignorance as to the nature and causes of anxiety-related problems leads a spouse or significant other to view the loved one as being "silly" or "childish." The result is that the spouse or significant other withdraws and ignores the problem or tries to "fix" the loved one by giving simplistic solutions that do not help. Both of these approaches weaken the relationship and cause anger and bitterness in the person who is suffering from the anxiety-related problems.

As you educate yourself, you may find that you are dealing with many issues similar to those of your loved one. When this is the case, sharing such a discovery can be very beneficial. It can also help you become more effective in your own life. One of the best ways to educate yourself is to become a study partner. If your personality or your relationship with your loved one makes this difficult, you can at least read this book and discuss what you have learned.

I encourage you to do the exercises yourself and discuss those sections of the book that describe issues with which you struggle.

For example, you can construct your own genogram as you work through chapter 2, and identify core beliefs and associations that interfere with your life as you work through chapter 4. Since much of what is written in this book applies to everyone, you may find that you and your loved one share many struggles of which you were unaware. Working through the book in this manner is a wonderful way to support your loved one, and will probably deepen the bond between you.

2

The Imprint of
Childhood

In this chapter you'll meet Mary, Robert, and Kimberly. Each one struggled with anxiety and achieved long-term recovery. The road they traveled is similar to the road that most of my clients have taken, regardless of their diagnoses. Although the problem you're confronting may be different from theirs, you'll probably find many areas in which their stories are similar to yours. Even if you don't, keep in mind that the purpose of following their journey is to extract principles that you can apply to your struggles.

Each of the following descriptions of Mary, Robert, and Kimberly is divided into four sections. The first section gives a brief client profile along with the initial description of the difficulties that person reported. This is followed by a *genogram*, a diagram of the members of the client's family. The squares in each genogram represent males, and the circles represent females. A horizontal line represents a marriage. A vertical zigzag line (such as the one in Robert's and Kimberly's genograms) represents a divorce. The vertical lines drawn to Mary, Robert, and Kimberly are a little longer than those drawn to their brothers and sisters. This is simply to make them stand out from their siblings.

Mary is the youngest child in her family, while Robert and Kimberly are both the eldest children. In addition to their parents, the genograms include adults who played an active role in their lives while they grew up. In Mary's case these were her maternal grandmother and grandfather, as well as her uncle. In Kimberly's case this included her stepfather.

Following each genogram is a brief description of each adult and a set of early recollections from the client's grade school, middle school, and high school years.

Mary

Mary is an attractive woman in her late twenties, of average height, with a slender, athletic build. She is divorced and works as a secretary in a state government agency. She began our first session by stating that while she had only occasional "major" panic attacks, she was experiencing high levels of anxiety and worry on a daily basis. Mary had been battling anxiety for almost five years. She had seen a couple of therapists and had experienced some relief. Lately, however, her symptoms were again getting worse. She did not travel very far from where she lived, and usually avoided theaters, restaurants, and social gatherings where more than two or three people were present.

Mary is a long-distance runner but could no longer run in the foothills where she loved to train. She reported that her symptoms began when she was traveling and had to take an airplane during a storm. On her next trip, a short time later, she again experienced intense anxiety. After this, she began to experience panic attacks more frequently and in more situations. Her condition was initially diagnosed as panic disorder with agoraphobia.

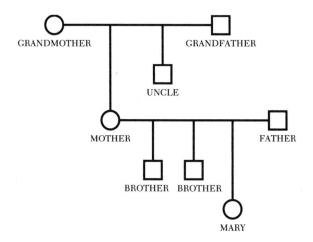

The Adults in Mary's Childhood

Mother:

> Mom was a secretary in my grade school. She was a very critical person and always seemed anxious. She would not drive when it was dark, and I believe she's an alcoholic. She begins sipping wine around dinnertime and sort of "zones out" for the evening. She was fairly distant when I was young, although we have become somewhat closer as I've grown older.

Father:

> Dad was a truck driver, so he was gone a lot. He always seemed to be angry about something. He was an only child, and I think this is why he was fairly self-cen-

tered. I remember that he controlled the house. However, I think he was a good father. I knew he loved me even though he never said it, and he made sure we had whatever we needed. I was his "little princess" when I was young and couldn't wait for him to come home from his trips. I always wanted to please him. He took us to parks on Sunday, which became a high point for me throughout my younger years.

Grandfather:

Grandfather was definitely an alcoholic. While I didn't know him very well, from what I've heard he was a very troubled man. He killed himself with poison. Unfortunately, he didn't take enough to kill himself quickly, and he suffered a long, miserable death. He was a nervous man. I've heard stories that he stopped driving when he was in his fifties. He told everyone that cars were going just too fast for him.

Grandmother:

As with my grandfather, Grandmother was just sort of in the background. We would visit periodically and she would always be busy in the kitchen or cleaning something. I liked her because she always had a hug and something sweet for me to eat.

Uncle:

My uncle came by every now and then. I remember that when he came we would go out to eat and we had a good time. There was a lot of talking and joking. Dad seemed to like him a lot. I was always proud to tell everyone he was my Uncle Jake.

Mary's Early Recollections

Preschool through Grade School:

I was terrified the first few weeks of kindergarten. I don't remember why, but for some reason I refused to tie my shoes throughout all of kindergarten. During grade school I often thought my friends were talking about me and that they felt sorry for me. I would do anything to please my teachers. I felt unloved, and spent a lot of time playing with make-believe friends until about the first grade. I remember lots of punishment from Mom. She would spank or slap us and put Tabasco sauce or soap in my mouth whenever she thought I was "talking back." I was a "cry baby" and would cry over almost anything. My brothers teased and ridiculed me a lot. Sometimes they were very cruel. I felt like a burden to my mother because I once heard her saying that I was "unplanned." I can remember never feeling safe except when I would hide in the back of my closet and cover myself with dirty clothes.

Middle School:

I became active in sports and found that this was an area where I could do well. I liked track and field, and began running. I had friends but none were really close friends. I always had the feeling of being on the outside looking in. I tended to devote my time to running and schoolwork. As a result, I did well in school.

High School:

High school was more of the same. I continued to run, dated some, and had friends, but I always felt like I never really connected with anyone.

Early Adult:

My marriage was fairly good during the early years. I was happy at last and felt like I had found my niche. Then, when the anxiety began, things started going downhill. At first, my husband tried to understand and was supportive. But, eventually I think he just got fed up with all of my worry and anxiety, and decided to call it quits. We divorced about two years ago. Since there were no children we just split everything up and went our separate ways.

Robert

Robert had just turned forty when he came to our first session. He is about five feet six inches tall, married for the second time, and has one child, a son from his first marriage. Robert was experiencing extreme anxiety almost constantly. He was the supervisor of a very stressful unit in a manufacturing plant and was just barely able to function there. In addition to experiencing major panic attacks at work and very high levels of anxiety, he had an unusual gag response that prevented him from eating anything except soup and baby food.

Robert reported that his symptoms began four years earlier while he was on a business trip. He had a severe case of flu and happened to choke on some food at a restaurant. His initial diagnosis was also panic disorder with agoraphobia because, like Mary, he was experiencing frequent panic attacks and avoidance patterns. Since doctors could find no medical reason for Robert's unusual gag response, and it seemed connected with the stress he was experiencing, a secondary tentative diagnosis of conversion disorder was also made. A conversion disorder refers to a physical response that is generated by psychological rather than physiological causes. Essentially, it's a representation of or a reaction to inner psychological conflict.

In Robert's genogram, the vertical zigzag line indicates that Robert's parents divorced when he was eighteen. He has a younger sister.

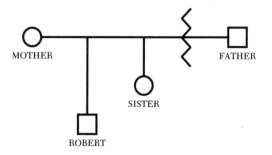

The Adults in Robert's Childhood

Mother:

Mother was born in another country and married Dad while he was stationed overseas. She was a very emotional person. Sometimes she would explode and call me or other family members names when they did something to displease her. Other times she would burst into tears. She had a very hard life when she was little and was not very well educated. She was a very negative person and not too close to us emotionally. She did not work outside of home. In fact, her main focus in life was home. During high school I thought of her as Alice in Wonderland because she seemed to live in her own little world and never really knew what was going on in the lives of the people around her. Our home always looked great and we were always well dressed and neat. Someone looking at us from the outside probably thought we were a great family because we always looked so good.

Father:

Father was an electrical engineer. He was an alcoholic and drank several beers every night while sitting in front of the television. He would drink two or three six-packs on the weekend. It seemed like we were always running out of beer. Father was a very intense person who was often violent. About once a week he and Mother would get into an argument and he would end up hitting her. Sometimes he would hit us. I remember that everything had to be his way or no way. There was always a "correct" way to do everything.

Robert's Early Recollections

Preschool through Grade School:

One of my earliest memories is when I was at dinner and started choking. I thought, "I can't let anyone see this." Father saw I was having trouble and helped me dislodge the piece of food that was stuck in my throat. Afterward, no one said anything and they just went on with dinner as if nothing had happened. I wasn't very happy as a kid. I was always on edge. At night, there was the fear of being beaten by dad. Then during the day I was picked on by bullies at school and afraid that they would beat me. I was a weakling and always hiding how I felt. We lived outside of the United States during most of my younger years. I was in Indiana when I was two. First grade was spent in Pakistan, then we came back to the states. From the fourth grade through middle school we lived in Japan.

Middle School:

This was a terrible time in my life. I was very small, and several bullies in the class made beating me up their purpose in life. I had few friends. Academically, I was an average student and got Bs and Cs.

High School:

I was still the smallest kid in my high school. However, we were now living in the United States, so I seemed to fit in better. I developed a circle of friends and continued to be an average student with Bs and Cs.

Early Adult:

Nothing too outstanding happened to me. I went to college and got a business administration degree. My first marriage lasted ten years and was fairly rocky. I followed my father's pattern and was quite the bully in the early years of my first marriage. Although I changed a lot during those ten years, my wife remained full of bitterness because of the early years. I don't think she ever saw the changes I made. We finally divorced but stayed on reasonable terms because of our son. We both want to do what's right for him, so we communicate well in that area. I met my second wife at work, and the marriage would be great if it weren't for this problem I have with choking. It's creating a lot of tension between us.

Kimberly

Kimberly is a tall, somewhat heavy woman in her late thirties with a very effervescent personality. She is divorced and has two sons who live with her. Kimberly works as a school district nurse, helping disabled students who have severe medical and emotional problems. As we talked, she told me how, about six months earlier, she had been attacked by one of the students under her care. During the assault she was hurt very severely, and she was now having very intense episodes of anxiety during the day and nightmares of the incident at night. She was always "on guard" and avoided parks, convenience stores, and many other places where she feared she might be attacked.

Kimberly took a medical leave for about a month after the incident and then an unpaid leave because she felt she could not

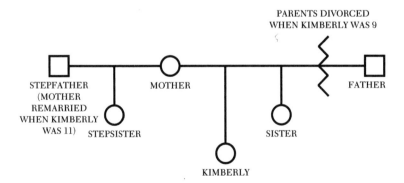

go back. She was initially diagnosed as having posttraumatic stress disorder.

The Adults in Kimberly's Childhood

Mother:

Mother was a beautician/hairdresser. She was a beautiful woman and an excellent mom. Our home was always neat and clean. She was always there for us when we needed anything for school. She was always easy to talk to and we have always been very close.

Father:

Father was a high school P.E. teacher. He was kind of like a drill sergeant: demanding, unforgiving, dogmatic, and a perfectionist. Nothing ever seemed to please him. I never had any real relationship with him. We were always competing. We were an active family and did lots of things such as fishing, volleyball, and so on. However, there was always this fierce competition to see who would get the biggest fish or win at a game. He never said, "I love you," and there was never any real demonstration of love. I continued to see my birth father after Mother remarried, and I love him very much. However, our relationship has always been one long contest.

Stepfather:

My stepfather managed a large chain grocery store. He was friendly and much more even tempered than my birth father. We got along well, and by the time I entered high school I was much closer to him than to my birth father. He was a real anchor for me during my teenage years.

Kimberly's Early Recollections

Preschool through Grade School:

My childhood was good. I was happy and had lots of friends. I liked school and did well, getting Bs and As. We were a very active family. We played all kinds of sports and went camping at least twice a year. There were no major traumas during childhood—just this constant competition with my father. I think he was disappointed at having only girls. I think that's why I was so into sports. It was a way for me to connect with Dad. My large size helped me compete. The only negative note was that Dad was so hard to please. I think I made up for it by becoming very close to my mother.

Middle School:

For the most part I enjoyed middle school. I continued to be active in sports. However, it's difficult being tall at this age. I was six feet tall in the seventh grade and was self-conscious about my height, especially around boys who were much shorter than I was. I was a good student and got Bs and As. My size made me a great competitor in sports.

High School:

I became less active in sports and turned my attention more to academics and drama. I loved to sing and did very well in school. By the tenth grade there were enough boys I knew in my grade or grades above mine who were as tall as I was so that I wasn't feeling like such a freak. However, I did get a lot of ribbing and heard all of the tall jokes that have ever been thought of. All in all, however, I had a pretty good time in high school.

Early Adult:

I enjoyed nursing school even though it was difficult. I met my husband and we had two sons fairly early in the marriage. I worked part-time when they were small. I began working full-time at my current position in the school district about six years ago and have always felt like I was making a real contribution. Until the assault, I was never worried about the kids and felt like I could handle anything.

Even a cursory glance at the above brief descriptions suggests that Mary, Robert, and Kimberly each carried baggage from childhood into adulthood. As each talked about his or her childhood experiences, this became even more evident.

Summary of Key Ideas

1. As you follow the stories of Mary, Robert, and Kimberly, look for principles you can apply to your struggle with anxiety.
2. Construct a genogram that includes descriptions of the adults in your life during your childhood. Then list early recollections from grade school, middle school, high school, and your adult life.

Recommended Activities

Construct a Genogram of Your Family

Using the models presented in this chapter, construct a genogram that shows your family when you were young. Just as Mary included her maternal grandmother, be sure to include grandparents, uncles, aunts, and anyone else who played a significant role during your developmental years. If you're in a close relationship with someone, whether it's someone you're married to or simply a boyfriend or girlfriend, make a second genogram of this person and his or her family. Use a full sheet of eight-and-a-half-by-eleven-inch paper to do this so you can include the descriptions of your parents and early recollections on the same sheet.

Write Descriptions of Your Parents

After you've completed your basic genogram, describe each of your parents and anyone else who played a significant role in raising you. Include a few words about their personalities. Were they easygoing, shy, critical, or outgoing? Also, include a few words about your relationship with them. Was it warm or cold, were they easy to talk to or distant? Some people find it helpful to pretend that they are writing a character description for an actor who is to play the role of a particular parent.

Write Descriptions of Your Childhood Experiences

After you've completed your descriptions of the adults who raised you, write a brief description of what it was like when you were very young (earliest memories through the sixth grade), during your middle-school years (seventh through ninth), high school years (tenth through twelfth), and adult years. Do not focus only on what is positive or negative. Instead, list ordinary recollections. The goal is to paint a portrait of what life was like for you in general during each of these periods of time.

What Are the Different Types of Anxiety-Related Problems?

If you've never read a description of the various anxiety-related problems, take a few minutes to read appendix 1. It gives a brief summary of the various anxiety disorders as they're currently defined. Mary's and Robert's diagnoses were panic disorder with agoraphobia. Kimberly's diagnosis was posttraumatic stress disorder.

3

The Time Tunnel

Most of my clients spend a lot of time puzzling over why they are struggling with anxiety. Questions such as "Why did this happen?" "What's wrong with me?" or "Why can't I just get over this?" occupy many of their waking hours. Because of this, it is important that they have reasonable and understandable answers for their "whys." Once they have answers, they can turn their attention to learning how to reduce their symptoms and moving toward long-term recovery.

In order to answer the question "Why do anxiety-related problems develop and continue to be a problem?" you need to know about conditioned responses, a phenomenon I call "time tunneling," and how emotions work. The material in this chapter and the next covers these topics and is the same information I covered with Mary, Robert, Kimberly, and hundreds of others as the first step on the road to recovery.

Conditioned Responses

At the turn of the century, a Russian scientist named I. P. Pavlov conducted what is now considered a classic experiment. He presented a neutral stimulus such as a ringing bell to hungry dogs, then followed it by giving the animals food. The food caused the dogs to salivate. With repetition, the neutral stimulus (the bell) became associated with the food and would, by itself, cause salivation. This type of conditioning is called a *conditioned response*.

Many human reactions and behaviors are a type of conditioned response. Consider the saying "Mom's cooking tastes best." Mom could be a terrible cook and the saying would still be true because her children would have been conditioned to her cooking. This explains why food in foreign countries often tastes "funny." The same is true with clothing fashions. Pictures of clothes worn ten years ago look odd because we have been slowly reconditioning ourselves to the fashions of today. In fact, many daily activities such as driving a car have a host of conditioned responses associated with them. Without these patterns we couldn't function in daily life.

Posttraumatic Stress Disorder

While conditioned responses play an important role in all forms of anxiety-related problems, they are easiest to understand in posttraumatic stress disorder. Posttraumatic stress disorder is the term psychology uses to describe the symptoms that a person experiences after a severe trauma. During World War I, posttraumatic stress disorder was referred to as shell shock; during World War II it was called battle fatigue. Today, the posttraumatic stress disorder model is applied to any situation where a normal person goes through an abnormal and traumatic experience such as rape, assault, a natural disaster, major surgery, or wartime combat duty, or suffers or witnesses a serious accident.

A person with posttraumatic stress disorder can experience recurring images of the traumatic event, a feeling that the traumatic event is occurring in the present, recurring distressing dreams of the trauma, or intense physical discomfort when exposed to events that symbolize or resemble an aspect of the traumatic event. This person may avoid places or things associated with the trauma, or they may experience a general numbing that can range from avoidance of thoughts or feelings associated with the trauma to a general feeling of detachment or estrangement from others. There are also usually two or more forms of body arousal present that can range from irritability and difficulty falling asleep or staying asleep to outbursts of anger and an exaggerated startle response.

Kimberly presents a vivid example of posttraumatic stress disorder. After her assault, driving by the school or thinking about returning to work would frequently trigger what are often called "flashbacks," episodes where Kimberly would reexperience the assault in various ways. Sometimes the incident would replay in her mind in such a clear and vivid manner that she felt as if the assault were actually occurring again. Other times she became anxious when an adolescent similar in appearance to the person who assaulted her passed her in a store or on the street.

It is important to understand posttraumatic stress disorder because of the type of conditioned responses that develop during trauma. When you think you are in danger, whatever sensory stimulation is occurring at that time—sights, sounds, odors, tactile sensations—tends to trigger what is commonly called the "fight-or-flight" mechanism in your body whenever you encounter that stimulation in the future. It makes no difference whether the danger is real or imaginary. The more intensely you perceive the danger, the stronger the effect. This response has been very important for human survival, especially when we lived in more primitive conditions. If a certain sight, sound, smell, or touch meant danger, people had to respond immediately in order to survive. This response still helps people respond quickly to danger whether they are in a war zone or simply driving to work.

There is no logical thinking associated with conditioned responses. They are automatic, *unconscious* reactions. A simple way to understand this is to pretend that you are connected to a device that can give you an electric shock, and that I will administer that shock every time I say the word *purple*. If I continue to do this, you will begin to twitch whenever I say, "purple." Then, even though I disconnect the wires, destroy the device, and explain that you will not be shocked anymore, I can still say the word *purple* and you will twitch.

This is an important point because much of the popular psychology found in self-help books aimed at the general public today is *insight oriented*. This means that the authors of such books concentrate on explaining why you act and feel the way you do. The assumption is that once you understand the causes of a problem, the problem will disappear. Unfortunately, while insight is useful, *insight alone usually does not change the way a person thinks and acts.*

This does not mean that insight is worthless. Insight and knowledge have an important place, as can be seen in the example of playing a musical instrument. If you don't know the basic principles of musical notation and proper fingering, you cannot practice correctly. While insight and knowledge alone do not provide you with the *skills* you need, they are a necessary first step.

Now let's return to the electric shock example. If I continue to say "purple" over and over without giving you a shock, you will stop twitching after some time has passed. You will become *desensitized* to the word. Indeed, this is what happened in Kimberly's case. Over time she again became comfortable in the various situations that had been triggering symptoms when she first came to see me. This is the second point about conditioned responses. It is possible to desensitize yourself so that a stimulus or "trigger" will no longer set off a conditioned response. This is one of the tasks covered in detail in the chapters that follow.

The Time Tunnel

When people respond to the present as if they were in the past, I refer to them as being in the "time tunnel." Time tunneling is a type of conditioned response that helps explain why people who were raised in troubled homes often find themselves trapped in dysfunctional patterns. Robert is a good example. The physical and verbal abuse from his father, the verbal abuse from his mother, and the threat of being beaten up in school became so deeply embedded a conditioned response that it followed him into his adult life. Whenever he was around anyone who "felt" like his parents, he would react as he had when he was a child.

This conditioned response became particularly troublesome at work. Whenever Robert had a meeting with his supervisor, who happened to be abrasive and sometimes unreasonable, he would not speak up or confront the supervisor, and he often agreed to things he later regretted. When Robert left meetings with his supervisor, he was often filled with feelings of disgust and self-loathing. What was happening was simple. Whenever he was around his supervisor, the strong conditioning that took place when he was a boy was triggered by the supervisor, who "felt" like Robert's father. Because his father was dangerous, Robert had learned to keep quiet and avoid conflict. As an adult, Robert confused the past with the present without even knowing it. He was caught in the time tunnel every time he met with his supervisor.

Escaping the Time Tunnel

Learning the principles for escaping from the time tunnel is simple, although much time and effort usually are required before old patterns fade and are replaced with new ones.

The first step in escaping the time tunnel is to identify specific feelings, thoughts, or behaviors that indicate you are experiencing the present as if it were the past and repeating old patterns. Once you have identified these patterns, you will find yourself becoming more and more aware of them. The second step is to reorient yourself to the present whenever you see yourself repeating patterns from the past. A simple way to do this is to:

- State what is happening
- State what is real

Robert began to use this approach by identifying meetings with his supervisor as situations that often drew him into the time tunnel. Once he realized that he was reacting to his supervisor as if he were still a little boy in the presence of his angry father, he began using this approach to keep himself in the present. For example, just before going into a meeting with his supervisor, Robert found it valuable to repeat the following lines to himself: "I'm starting to go through the time tunnel. The feelings I'm experiencing are responses from the past. They were appropriate when I was little. Now it's time to come back to the present. My supervisor is *not* my father. He is just my supervisor. I am *not* a helpless little boy trapped at home anymore. I am an adult with lots of skills and abilities. I'm not going to get beaten up. I'm just going to have a routine discussion of job assignments in my unit."

At first, Robert had to repeat these statements several times to himself prior to a meeting with his supervisor, and sometimes during the meeting. As he did this, he found it easier and easier to react to his supervisor in a more adult manner. As Robert became more skilled at staying in the present with his supervisor, he began to notice when he became anxious and fidgety around certain other people when there was no reason to be anxious. He identified these people as being similar to one of his parents in some way and throwing him back into the past. Sometimes it was the person's voice. Other times it was the person's appearance or position.

Robert also realized that situations where he was criticized often triggered childhood patterns he had developed in response to his critical mother. In his first marriage, he became very angry whenever his wife criticized him. Even simple comments triggered explosive anger. This eventually caused his first wife to leave him. In his second marriage he controlled his anger by swallowing it and remaining calm on the outside. This eventually turned out to be one of the factors behind his gagging problem.

Four Common Traits in Adults with Abusive Childhoods

There are four common traits found in adults who have been abused as children. A person who has experienced severe sexual, physical, or emotional abuse will usually have all four. A person who experienced limited abuse will probably have only some of the traits, and those that are present will interfere with this person's life in only a limited number of situations.

The first trait is the *tendency to be triggered by specific events,* which has been called time tunneling in this chapter. Mary, Robert, and Kimberly each experienced anxiety that was triggered by situations and events that resembled childhood experiences. Because Kimberly's background was much less severe than Mary's or Robert's, she had the least amount of difficulty in this area.

The second trait is *difficulty modulating emotions.* This means that it is easy for a person to become anxious or angry, and, once angered or frightened, it is difficult for this person to calm down. This is especially true when events trigger time tunneling, where the exaggerated danger and helplessness a person experienced as a child has been transposed into their present situation. In addition, time tunneling tends to trigger some age regression, which reduces a person's ability to reason and manage emotions.

An adult who had to suppress many emotions as a child may also find it difficult to feel emotions at a low level because the tendency to suppress emotions has become automatic. In this person, emotions are felt only when they are very strong. Thus, this person either experiences too much of an emotion or nothing at all. Robert, for example, might sometimes feel intense hatred toward a stranger, but at the same time, might discuss a very intense issue with his wife in a flat and emotionless manner.

The third trait is a *tendency to view oneself and the world negatively.* The three key areas affected are the ability to trust, feel safe, and believe that it is possible to bring about desired outcomes. Two key areas in terms of one's self-image are whether or not one is normal and whether or not one is lovable. This is discussed in detail in the next chapter.

The nature of the abuse can greatly affect the form of these negative views. For instance, if a person was abused by a stranger, he or she may feel a sense of safety when close to loved ones, and a sense of danger when far away from them. However, if a person was abused by someone who was supposed to protect and give love, the identification of what and who are "safe" becomes confused.

The fourth trait is a *reduced ability to understand events*. People with this tendency find that they often go into a daze or become confused, especially when they are stressed, dealing with conflict, or emotionally upset. When a child is being abused and cannot escape physically, the child often takes the only other form of escape possible: *dissociation*. Dissociation is the ability to remove oneself mentally from a situation. The more frequent and severe the abuse, the greater the tendency to remove oneself mentally from the painful experience. Unfortunately, this automatic habit pattern often continues into adulthood. This causes the person to dissociate whenever a current event feels like pain from the past.

These tendencies can create many different types of problems. For example, people with abusive childhoods often find it difficult to distinguish unhealthy individuals from healthy ones. Their childhood experiences taught them to ignore the important indicators that to those raised in healthy families became danger signals. Instead, they "numb out" or use an old response pattern that causes them to walk into harm's way without even knowing it.

These tendencies can greatly affect a person's spiritual side. It is difficult to find satisfying answers to questions such as "Is there a God?" "Is there a larger meaning to life?" and "Is it worth giving a part of myself to others?" In addition, an abused child often develops a self-concept that contains beliefs about being dirty, inadequate, guilty, or responsible for what happened. As a result, a person like this often makes up a "cover story" and tries to hide who he or she really is. All of this makes it difficult for him or her to develop healthy relationships and function effectively.

Summary of Key Ideas

1. Conditioned responses are automatic, unconscious reactions that play a major role in all human behavior.
2. Conditioned responses play a major role in all anxiety-related problems. This is easiest to see in posttraumatic stress disorder.
3. While insight is useful, insight alone usually does not change the way a person thinks and acts.
4. It is possible to desensitize yourself to the triggers associated with conditioned responses.
5. Time tunneling refers to times when a person responds to the present as if it were the past.
6. To escape time tunneling and return to the present, state what is happening, then state what is real.
7. Adults who have been abused as children often have (1) a tendency to be triggered by specific events, (2) difficulty modulating emotions, (3) a tendency to view themselves and the world negatively, and (4) a reduced ability to understand events.

Recommended Activities

Identify Triggers That Cause You to
Time Tunnel

This chapter describes the source of problem behaviors that tend to be the most difficult to change: the automatic patterns you learned while growing up. While they are not the only factors, they do play a major role in most anxiety-related problems. Be sure to allow time to systematically work through the recommended activities in the chapters that follow.

Review the genogram, the descriptions of the adults who raised you, and the early recollections you completed at the end of chapter 2. Identify as many childhood patterns as you can that you still repeat today. Keep in mind that *the solutions of childhood are often the problems of adulthood.* Whenever you notice yourself reacting to the present as if it were the past, use the simple approach of stating what's happening and what's real to reorient yourself to the present. It is also useful to use this approach when you are about to enter a situation that often causes you to time tunnel so you can stay in the present.

Begin Keeping a Journal

Begin keeping a journal. Use your journal to complete the written activities, list problems and concerns, record insights, and keep track of your progress. As the chapters unfold, you will find that your journal is an extremely effective tool for growth. You don't need to use anything expensive or fancy. A simple spiral-bound notebook is fine. Some people prefer a three-ring binder, to which paper can be added. A few like the feel of a more expensive bound book with blank pages. You decide which is most comfortable for you.

As you work with your journal, keep in mind that privacy is essential. This makes it easier to write honestly and openly. Do not write for an "unseen audience"; the need to please these invisible watchers will cause you to lose much of the benefit of keeping a journal.

The main value of a journal is not the permanent record you create but the work required to create it. After several months you may decide to destroy your journal or keep it as a source of encouragement for the progress it records.

A Word about Sleep

When you are not sleeping well, your body becomes more reactive and your ability to think clearly is reduced. Chronic sleep problems can cause your symptoms to escalate and interfere with your ability to learn the skills described in this book. In fact, clients with poor sleep habits often find that simply improving the quality of their sleep significantly reduces their symptoms.

Since chronic sleep disorders can be caused by many different medications and physical problems, it is always best to discuss sleep problems with your physician. If they are a major issue, you may even want to consult a physician who specializes in sleep disturbances.

Fortunately, many sleep problems are simply due to poor sleep habits or to thinking patterns that interfere with sleep. Here are several suggestions for developing what is commonly called good *sleep hygiene:*

- *Establish a regular time to go to bed and get up.* Avoid making up for lost sleep on weekends or holidays. If you have been going to bed and getting up at widely varying times, you may need to reset your biological clock by following a regular schedule for sleep. It is alright to take naps if they are taken on a fixed schedule and you make appropriate adjustments to your nighttime schedule.
- *Reserve your bed for sleeping and sex.* Watching television, reading, or doing other activities in bed is one of the most common reasons for difficulty in falling asleep. If you are finding it very difficult to sleep well, make the bedroom off-limits to everything except sleep and sex.
- *Create a proper environment for sleep.* People often forget

about obvious things such as making sure the bedroom is dark, quiet, and well ventilated.

- *Develop a routine that prepares you for sleep.* This routine becomes a conditioned response trigger that tells your body, "It's time to fall asleep." A typical routine might include brushing your hair and teeth, pulling down the sheets, and setting out clothes for the next day.
- *For two hours prior to sleeping, restrict your activities to those that are relaxing.* These activities might include taking a hot bath or shower, reading, watching television, praying, and meditating. Avoid anxiety-provoking activities like paying bills or arguing.
- *Use relaxation-response techniques.* Many find that breath counting is especially useful. See appendix 4 for an explanation of this and other techniques.
- *If you've been lying awake for twenty minutes, get up.* If you have spent twenty minutes using one of the relaxation-response exercises in appendix 4 and are still awake, get up and go to a different part of the house. Do a relaxing activity such as reading a book or watching television until you feel tired. You may at first find yourself spending much of the night out of bed, and get only four or five hours of sleep altogether, but these short periods of continuous, sound sleep will gradually expand to fill the night.
- *Avoid caffeine, nicotine, heavy meals, and strenuous exercise for three to five hours before bedtime.*
- *Exercise during the day.* Exercising in the late afternoon increases the amount of deep sleep you get in the first half of the night. Even a brisk walk around the block may help. However, exercise just before sleeping interferes with sleep.
- *Create "noise screens."* If noise in your surroundings makes it difficult for you to go to sleep or wakes you up, block out the noise with a noise screen. One way to do this is to place

a radio next to your bed and tune it *between* stations to produce *white noise,* which will mask other sounds. Some people find that earplugs or a combination of earplugs and white noise helps.

- *Stay away from alcohol.* Even moderate amounts of alcohol can disturb sleep or create a backlash of sleeplessness later in the night that makes sleep problems worse.
- *Avoid using sleeping medications regularly.* Over-the-counter remedies (usually antihistamines) are often not very effective. One exception seems to be *melatonin,* a relatively new product that can be purchased in health food stores. While early reports indicate that melatonin can be helpful, be sure to consult your physician before using it. Prescription drugs can alter normal sleep patterns and suppress deep sleep or REM (rapid eye movement) sleep—the time during sleep when you are dreaming. They can also leave you groggy the next day. Because the body becomes tolerant of some drugs, higher and higher doses are needed, leading to dependency. In fact, sleeping pills are often one of the main causes of long-term sleeplessness.
- *If you get drowsy during the day, change the pace of your activity.* The most "natural" way to keep awake is to move: Get up from your chair, pace the floor, and stretch. Try light rests and creative breaks instead of alcohol, cigarettes, or coffee.

If worrying about problems makes it difficult for you to fall asleep or keeps you awake in the middle of the night, try the following:

- Get out of bed and go to another part of the house. Develop a concrete plan for dealing with the problem and write it down on a piece of paper. After you've developed your plan, write a one- or two-sentence summary of what you are going to do.
- If you are drowsy when you complete your plan, go on to the next step. If you are not drowsy, do a relaxing activity to wind down.
- Go to bed and use one of the relaxation-response techniques described in appendix 4. Again, many people find breath counting especially effective.
- If you find yourself thinking about the problem, recite the one- or two-sentence summary you wrote and use a relaxation-response exercise to distract yourself.
- If worry over problems prior to going to sleep is a recurring pattern, establish a regular time at least two hours before your bedtime during which you think about your problems and develop concrete plans for dealing with them.

Some people are awakened by panic attacks in the middle of the night. Current research suggests that these *nocturnal panic attacks* are due to some neurological mechanism that is not understood at present. If you experience nocturnal panic attacks but are able to return to sleep fairly easily, continue to do whatever you do to return to sleep. However, if nocturnal panic attacks are triggering negative self-talk and high levels of anxiety that make it difficult for you to return to sleep, do the following:

- Prepare an index card with coping statements such as "These nocturnal panic attacks are due to a neurological quirk. They are *not* dangerous. The uncomfortable feelings they generate are uncomfortable, but they last only a little while. Find something relaxing to do until you feel drowsy. Then, go back to bed and use your relaxation-response exercise." After you've made your index card, place it beside your bed or in your bathroom.

- When you experience a nocturnal panic attack, get up and wash your face so you become fully awake. Once you're fully awake, read the card you've prepared.

- Next, spend about five to twenty minutes with a distracting and relaxing activity that allows your body to settle down, such as reading a book or having a cup of warm milk (avoid cocoa since it has caffeine in it).

- Finally, when you begin to feel drowsy, go back to bed. If you are still a little restless, use one of the relaxation-response techniques in appendix 4 to help you get back to sleep.

A Word for People with Severe Symptoms

If your symptoms are severe and seriously interfere with your life, seek professional help. Methodologies such as eye movement desensitization and reprocessing (EMDR) can be very useful. However, they do require you to work with a trained therapist. Appendix 2 discusses this and other forms of help in more detail.

4

The Mystery of Emotions

Anxiety is a basic emotion that humans experience on a daily basis. In order to understand how anxiety can change from a mild everyday occurrence into an uncontrollable nightmare, you need a general understanding of emotions. Once you understand how emotions work, you will be ready to gain a full understanding of the dynamics that lead to anxiety-related problems. This understanding is the foundation for achieving long-term recovery.

Emotions can be very mysterious. They often come and go with no apparent reason. They can make life wonderful or miserable. The importance of emotions to our experience is seen by the fact that throughout the ages in all cultures, emotional conflict is a key component of all good drama and theater. You can also find scores of books dealing with various aspects of emotions filling the self-help section of bookstores. Yet most people have little understanding as to *how* emotions work and *why* we have them.

The confusion and mystery surrounding emotions are caused by the way in which we talk *about* them without ever really defining what we are talking about. When I lead workshops for therapists, I often start with two questions: "What are emotions?" and "What is their function?" It's amazing how many therapists complete their training without developing a clear answer to these two questions. In light of this confusion in the therapeutic community, it's no wonder that emotions are so bewildering to the average person. In this chapter, I provide the answers I've developed as the result of years of studying research on emotions and working with people.

What Are Emotions?

In everyday language we speak of emotions as if they were a specific *thing*. But emotions are not a specific thing. Instead, emotions are a *complex process with both biological and mental components*. Emotions are mental in that they usually are triggered by an *interpretation* of an event, which then produces a complex series of biochemical reactions we describe as a "feeling." The biochemical reactions also generate an "urge for action." Sometimes, the action you take in response to an emotion is mental, such as when you disagree with someone but decide not to say or do anything. Other times, it involves both thought and physical action, such as telling someone what you want or getting something you need. This process can be diagramed as follows:

Event → Interpretation → Emotion → Action

The above model is called a *cognitive model of emotions* (cognitive refers to thinking) because it stresses the mental factors that generate emotions. While the *majority* of your emotions are generated through the cognitive process diagramed above, there are some important exceptions. Many diseases, chemicals, injuries, and genetic defects can be the primary source of emotional responses. A few examples would be mood-altering drugs that can produce a wide range of inappropriate emotions, thyroid problems that cause anxiety, head trauma that causes excessive emotional outbursts, and genetic defects that cause bipolar disorder or endogenous depression. There also seem to be some emotional responses that are "hard wired" into us. One is the excitement felt when seeing an attractive member of the opposite sex. Another is the "runner's high" that many athletes feel during intense exertion.

In addition to the above noncognitive sources of emotional responses, several common everyday physical factors such as hunger, fatigue, illness, or stress can affect the process that generates emotions on two fronts. They can interfere with your ability to process events mentally and with the biochemical processes that generate emotions.

Why Do We Have Emotions?

The key word to remember when answering the question "Why do we have emotions?" is *needs*. Emotions are generated in direct response to whether or not we perceive that a need has been met, a threat is present, or a loss has occurred or might occur (keep in mind that a threat or loss means that various needs may no longer be met).

In simplistic terms it works like this: A part of your mind constantly evaluates events in terms of your needs and wants. This process of assigning meaning to events is usually done automatically and unconsciously. If a need or want has been satisfied or may soon be satisfied, you experience the various positive emotions such as joy, excitement, or satisfaction. If a threat is present, you experience anger (ranging from irritation to rage) or fear (ranging from apprehension to panic). If you encounter a loss, depending on the nature of the loss, you experience sadness, grief, or depression. Of course, events are often complex. They can satisfy some needs and frustrate others. This is why you often experience conflicting emotions. This process of interpreting needs and wants can be diagramed as follows:

		↗ A need has been satisfied or may be satisfied	→	Various positive emotions such as joy, excitement, or satisfaction
Event →	Interpretation →	A threat exists or may soon exist	→	Anger or Fear
		↘ A loss of some sort has occurred or may occur	→	Sadness, grief, or depression

Emotions trigger three types of action: behaviors, mental activity, and nonverbal communication. It is usually easy to identify the behaviors and thoughts that an emotion generates. However, most people don't associate the idea of communication with emotions. However, the nonverbal communication that results from changes in facial expression, body posture, and tone of voice are an important part of the action generated by emotions.

A simple exercise illustrates this point. Say the phrase "I love you" as if you were speaking to your lover. Now say it as if you are asking a question. Finally, in a lighthearted manner as if you were speaking in a casual manner to an acquaintance. Each evokes subtle changes in your facial expression, posture, and tone of voice that make the meaning clear to the other person without any further explanation. The changes that take place in you as your emotions change and others' ability to recognize them are, in essence, hard wired into us, making emotions a powerful form of communication.

All of these different components of emotions can be diagramed as follows:

Event →	Interpretation: →	Emotion:	→ Action
	1) Satisfaction of a need	1) Subjective feeling	1) Conscious or unconscious behavior
	2) Threat	2) "Urge" to take action	2) Thoughts associated with the need
	3) Loss	3) Physiological (body) responses	3) Nonverbal communication

Kimberly presents a good example of how all of these components work together. She longed for a permanent relationship and periodically would meet someone she found attractive. As with most complex situations, there were many different interpretations occurring at the same time. There was the potential for satisfying a need along with the threat that she might be rejected. This, in turn, heightened the loss she felt because she was single. The emotions generated by these were a mixture of excitement, anxiety, and melancholy. The mental actions generated by these emotions were thoughts of hope and pleasurable fantasies as well as thoughts of dread and visions of being alone the rest of her life. The behaviors generated included steps taken to ensure that she could spend time with this person, as well as some avoidance in the form of acting shy and awkward. Her nonverbal communication included changes in the eyes, face, and body that are typical of a person who is deeply infatuated with someone.

Human Needs

There are many ways to group human needs. The simplest division found in general scientific research is to group needs into two categories: physical needs and psychological needs (which can also be referred to as mental needs). A third category often ignored is spiritual needs. To these three, I find it useful to add one other: relationship needs.

Physical Needs

This group of needs includes all of the physical things you *need to feel safe,* such as food, shelter, and freedom from harm.

Mental Needs

This is a rather broad range of needs relating to your *need to understand the world and how it works.* To keep things simple, I include several additional needs that are often listed separately. These include the need to explore and learn, and the need to create. Together they drive the desire to understand why people do the things they do and how you can accomplish the tasks you wish to complete.

Relationship Needs

Relationship needs can be summarized as your *need to have a deep connection to at least one other person.* In actuality, this need has physical, mental, and spiritual aspects. If a baby is not touched, it will not develop properly and may even die. Likewise, how you view yourself, others, and the world affects your ability to have and keep relationships.

Spiritual Needs

This group has to do with your *need to find meaning in both life and death*. Your spiritual needs cause you to seek answers to questions such as "Why am I here?" "What happens when I die?" "Does God exist?" People who do not believe in a soul or a spiritual dimension see spiritual questions as simply a special type of mental need. As such they seek answers to these questions only through philosophy and reason. If you belong to this group and do not like the term *spiritual,* you can think of these needs as existential needs since they deal with the problem of finding meaning for your existence.

Those who believe that there is a spiritual dimension both to the universe and to humans usually define this realm of needs in a metaphysical sense. They see these needs as transcending the purely physical and mental realities of science and touching on an aspect of the universe that does not fall within the purview of science. They believe that this area transcends mental and physical realities and is a separate and unique aspect of humans. For them, satisfying answers to questions concerning the meaning of life cannot be found in human reason alone. Instead, they can only be found from the experience of a relationship with God.

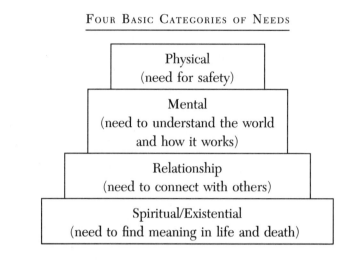

Physical
(need for safety)

Mental
(need to understand the world
and how it works)

Relationship
(need to connect with others)

Spiritual/Existential
(need to find meaning in life and death)

The needs in the above categories do not have to be met in any particular order to progress through them. For example, it is possible to satisfy one's physical needs without satisfying the need for relationship. Examples of this are easy to find. At the same time, people usually find there is a dissatisfaction and sense of restlessness in their lives when the needs in the lower blocks are not satisfied.

If you have a well-founded belief in who you are, your place in the world, and your purpose in life, it is easier to feel secure even when you are lacking physical necessities or suffering illness. When you have healthy, supportive relationships, you feel more secure about your place in the world even when going through transitions such as the loss of a job. Likewise, if you have no sense of purpose or a weak sense of who you are, you can have an abundance of things and be miserable except when sedated by temporary thrills. Without meaningful relationships, there will always be something missing in your ability to feel good about who you are and your purpose in life.

At the bottom of it all are your spiritual needs. Your answer to the question "What is the meaning of life?" plays an important role in determining your reaction to a host of normal and recurring life events.

Core Beliefs and Unconscious Associations

Everything you think is based on a set of beliefs that have been acquired over the course of your life. Because you think and speak in a type of shorthand, you are often unaware of many of the beliefs on which your thinking is based. One of the key features of *cognitive psychology*° is the identification of the beliefs that shape your interpretation of events, and that are the true source of most of your emotional responses.

There are simple practical beliefs about everyday events such as "water will come out of the shower when I turn it on," and what are often called *core beliefs:* beliefs about yourself, others, and reality that you can easily write down and that you believe to be true. I divide core beliefs into three general types: beliefs about yourself, beliefs about relationships, and beliefs about your place in the world. Here are examples of a positive and negative core belief in each area:

Beliefs about yourself:	"I have value" vs. "I am worthless"
Beliefs about relationships:	"Relationships can be very satisfying" vs. "People always leave me"

° Cognitive psychology focuses on your beliefs and how you think (your cognitions), as opposed to behavioral psychology, which focuses on behaviors, or psychodynamic psychology, which focuses on the interaction of conscious and unconscious mental or emotional processes within a person.

Beliefs about the world: "The world holds many opportunities" vs. "I can't win at anything"

In addition to these conscious beliefs, you have numerous *unconscious associations*. These associations are the result of groups of related conditioned responses that developed with specific people, situations, or needs during childhood and that then became associated in a more global way with some aspect of yourself, others, or the world in adulthood. These associations can be very different from your core beliefs and can also be thought of as "unconscious rules."

A simple, yet vivid, example of this type of association can be seen in Robert, who, when young, was physically, emotionally, and verbally abused. As a child, Robert quickly learned that his parents were dangerous and often caused him physical or emotional pain. As he became an adult, he found that it was very difficult for him to assert himself, especially with authority figures such as teachers or employers. The danger and fear associated with his parents had become associated with all authority figures. This association can be *labeled* as "people in authority are dangerous." When describing an association such as this with words, it is important to keep in mind that Robert did not come to this conclusion consciously. In fact, Robert was genuinely puzzled by his reaction to supervisors. His conscious belief was that he was a competent adult and there was no reason to be threatened by a superior.

Robert was responding to an *unconscious* association of all authority figures with his parents. As you will see in upcoming chapters, labeling these types of associations with descriptive phrases such as "people in authority are dangerous" provides you with a powerful tool for working with these patterns and defusing them.

We are now ready to place the final piece into the puzzle of emotions. You have already learned that part of your mind is always evaluating events in terms of whether your various needs will be met or frustrated. Your conscious beliefs *and* unconscious associations serve as the guiding forces that the mind uses in determining this. Sometimes you have associations that are in conflict with your beliefs, as shown in Robert's case. Whenever you experience an emotional reaction to an event that seems illogical or confusing, it is probably due to an interpretation that is based on one or more negative core beliefs or associations.

Summary of Key Ideas

1. Emotions are a complex process with biological and mental components.
2. The cognitive model of emotions sees emotions as being the result of your interpretation of events. This interpretation is often an unconscious process.
3. While the cognitive model explains how most everyday emotions are generated, there are important exceptions where emotions are generated through noncognitive means.
4. The function of emotions is to generate thoughts and actions that satisfy needs.
5. Satisfying a need generates positive emotions. Perceived or real threats generate anxiety or anger. Perceived or real losses generate sadness.
6. One way to view human needs is to divide them into four categories: physical, mental, relationship, and spiritual.
7. Core beliefs can be divided into three groups: beliefs about yourself, beliefs about relationships, and beliefs about your place in the world.
8. In addition to your conscious core beliefs, you have numerous

unconscious associations. These associations are the result of groups of related conditioned responses associated with specific people, situations, or needs during childhood becoming associated in a more global way with some aspect of yourself, others, or the world in adulthood.

9. Your unconscious associations or "unconscious rules" can be very different from your core beliefs. It is useful to label these associations so you can work with them consciously.

10. Your interpretation of events is based on a combination of conscious beliefs and unconscious associations.

Recommended Activities

Activity Overview: Lay a Strong Foundation

The information in this chapter is the foundation on which much of the material in the following chapters is based. Take your time with it. Be sure to reread it before going on to the next chapter. You may be surprised at what you missed the first time. If you find it difficult to understand, read it a third time. Just as the material in this chapter is designed to provide a foundation for the information in the chapters that follow, the recommended activities for this chapter are designed to prepare you for upcoming exercises. Both are essential for the work that is to come.

Identify Basic Concepts You Learned in Childhood

One of the key concepts in this chapter is the idea that emotions are triggered by an interpretation of events in terms of whether or not they meet or frustrate a need. Furthermore, this interpretation is based on conscious beliefs and unconscious associations. As you go through this exercise, keep in mind that it focuses on beliefs and associations that cause problems. In addition to negative beliefs and associations, Mary, Robert, and Kimberly also brought many positive beliefs out of childhood. For example, Mary's success in running and school helped her develop the belief and corresponding associations that "I can succeed if I work hard." Kimberly's close relationship with her mother and stepfather gave her the deep-seated belief and corresponding association "I'm loved and lovable." One of Robert's positive beliefs and associations was "I'm good with my hands." This was reflected in his skill with tools and working with mechanical things. When working with problem areas in your life, it's easy to forget that you also learned many positive things when you were young.

Keeping this in mind, here are some examples of *negative beliefs and associations* Mary, Robert, and Kimberly brought to their adult lives. Some, such as Mary's belief "I can't do anything right," are beliefs that were consciously held. Others, such as Robert's rule that "conflict is dangerous," were unconscious associations.

Mary

I can't do anything right.
I'm inferior to others. I'm not as intelligent or capable as
   they are.
When problems arise, don't look, don't feel, run away.
Love hurts, protect yourself.
The world is dangerous. I'm not safe.

Robert

Conflict is dangerous.
People in authority are dangerous.

Something is wrong with me. I'm inferior to others.
There's nothing I can do to make a difference.
People always let you down.
Numb yourself, don't feel anything.

Kimberly

Winning is what counts.
I have to be the best in order to have value.
Mistakes are not acceptable.
I must be strong and never show weakness.

The above are just partial lists of the problem beliefs and associations that were identified in these three individuals. However, they clearly show that Mary and Robert were very limited in their ability to form intimate relationships and deal with problems effectively. As you will see in the next few chapters, this played a major role in the development of their symptoms. Even Kimberly, who had a tremendous number of strengths that she brought from childhood, had one major weakness: the need never to make mistakes and always to be the best at whatever she did. While it's good to want to do well, Kimberly carried this desire to an extreme, where any mistake was a major defeat. This became a chief obstacle for her as she wrestled with recovering from the aftereffects of her assault.

While it is not too difficult to list your conscious negative beliefs about yourself, others, and the world, identifying unconscious associations is more difficult. Because they are the result of unconscious conditioned responses, you've probably never thought much about them. Fortunately, you can uncover them using a simple method based on the old adage "If it looks like a duck, talks like a duck, and walks like a duck, it's probably a duck." In cognitive psychology, this saying becomes "If you act like you believe something, speak like you believe something, and think like you believe something, you believe it." This belief is the unconscious association you are trying to identify.

In order to apply this principle to yourself, you need to have completed the exercises in chapter 2. If you have not completed them, stop and do so before you continue with this one. If you have completed the descriptions of your family and early childhood experiences, review them and make a list of those negative beliefs and associations that have caused you problems in life. The easiest way to do this is to review your genogram and the descriptions of your early childhood then ask yourself, "What kinds of beliefs and associations would a child growing up in this situation develop about him/herself, others, and the world?" Keep in mind the idea that "if you act, speak, or think like you believe something," that belief or association is probably playing an important role in your behavior whether you consciously agree with it or not. Here is a small sampling of the many different types of negative beliefs and associations about oneself, relationships, and the world that underlie dysfunctional behaviors.

Examples of Negative Beliefs and Associations about Yourself

I'm inferior to others (other ways of expressing this idea are: There is something wrong with me, I don't measure up, or I'm not as intelligent or capable as others).

I'm worthless.

I have no power. There's nothing I can do to make a difference in how events turn out.

I'm not lovable.

I'm dirty.

I'm ugly.
I'm a bad person.
I cannot succeed.
I'm incompetent.
I'm crazy.

Examples of Negative Core Beliefs and Associations about Relationships

Intimacy is dangerous (or results in pain), therefore, don't get close.
Conflict is dangerous.
People in authority are dangerous.
You can't trust anyone.
Sooner or later, people always abandon you.
The opposite sex is inferior/superior.
I'm responsible for how others feel.
If people see how I don't measure up, they will not like me.
Never discuss weaknesses, death, or illness with others. They might be hurt or think badly of you and leave you.

Examples of Negative Core Beliefs and Associations about the World

The world is fearful and dangerous.
There is no safe place in the world.
When bad things happen to me, it's my fault.
I have no power or control.
Life is meaningless.
To live is to suffer.
Illness and death are awful. Keep a close watch on your body because it is weak and fragile and something terrible can go wrong at any time.

If you find it difficult to identify your core beliefs and associations, you might find it useful to discuss this with someone you trust and who knows you well. Others often can see us more clearly than we can. If you don't have someone like this in your life, you might find it helpful to work with a trained therapist.

5

Developing Your Explanation for "Why"

To understand the dynamics that generate panic disorder, let's start by examining the initial onset of Mary's symptoms. As with most people, Mary's panic disorder developed in steps. It started when she experienced overwhelming anxiety and panic attacks aboard an airplane. As she prepared for her second plane trip, she began to engage in "negative anticipation" and "body scanning," which became primary forces for maintaining her severe anxiety. *Negative anticipation* is "what if" thinking. Because Mary didn't understand why she experienced such terrifying anxiety on her previous trip, she was apprehensive about her next plane flight. Her worry was characterized by thoughts such as:

"What if I panic on this flight?"
"What if I get so anxious I lose control?"
"What will people think?"
"Maybe I have some sort of 'mental problem.' "
"Maybe I have some sort of physical problem that my doctor missed."

These types of thoughts are a *normal and reasonable response* when frightening sensations are experienced for which there is no explanation. Having sound, reasonable answers for these types of questions that you understand and agree with helps you to stop this type of thinking. It also helps you shift your focus to the work of taking the necessary steps to achieve long-term recovery.

In addition to her negative anticipation, Mary began to do what is usually called *body scanning* or *internalization*. She began to monitor her body and look for signs that might indicate that the mysterious and terrifying symptoms were returning. As she waited for her flight, body scanning caused her to notice all sorts of sensations and reactions that she never noticed before. All of these reactions were normal, but, because she didn't understand them, she incorrectly identified them as signs that the terrible sensations she feared were returning.

As Mary boarded her flight and settled into her seat, her negative anticipation increased and triggered what is commonly known as the *fight-or-flight response*. This response is designed to decrease all of the reactions in the body that are not necessary for intense activity (such as digestion), and increase all of the reactions that are needed (such as increased heart rate, deeper breathing, sweating, and so on). As Mary noticed the increase in physical symptoms associated with the mysterious panic reaction, her fear increased, causing her symptoms to increase. This process is called the *anxiety/panic cycle* and can be diagramed as follows:

A normal reaction in the body	→ The reaction is noticed causing fear →	The fear triggers the fight-or-flight response
		↓
	The increased fear produces a ← stronger fight-or-flight response	The increased reaction in the body produces → more fear

Mary now entered the third stage of the process where the anxiety reaction becomes associated with more and more situations. Because the frightening reactions had occurred a second time without explanation, Mary began to worry and look for possible symptoms in her body in situations other than those associated with flying. For example, one morning during a routine run, she noticed what she thought was a little dizziness. This was actually a *normal* out-of-breath sensation that anyone who exercises intensely experiences. In the past she never paid much attention to it, but because she had become very worried about any unusual sensations, this frightened her and she once again talked herself into a *self-generated* panic attack. Soon she was monitoring her body all of the time.

When a person begins monitoring her body as closely as Mary did, she starts to notice all sorts of sensations and bodily reactions that were previously overlooked. Because these sensations seem to be new, the person wrongly assumes that they indicate some sort of disease process or abnormal reaction. In truth, the vast majority of the sensations that people report to me are simply *normal* reactions that were ignored prior to the onset of their symptoms.

For many people, the process of worrying and watching their bodies for signs of the dreaded symptoms soon takes on a life of its own. At this point, the conditioned responses discussed in chapter 3 play an important role in the development of their symptoms. In Mary's case, because she mistakenly associated danger with the normal sensations of running, these sensations became a conditioned-response trigger for anxiety. In fact, with time, just thinking about running would trigger mild anxiety. When Mary noticed this mild anxiety, she would begin the anxiety/panic cycle and sometime increase her anxiety until it became a panic attack.

For Robert, the association of danger with eating became such a strong conditioned response that just thinking of eating would trigger high levels of anxiety for him. Again, it should be pointed out that the initial anxiety generated by this type of conditioned response is completely unconscious. Once you've associated danger with a situation, activity, or bodily sensation, whenever it is experienced, it generates anxiety. A conditioned response like this will become extinguished in time *if* it is not reinforced with negative self-talk. Unfortunately, most people with anxiety-related problems do not understand this. Whenever they experience this type of conditioned response anxiety, they reinforce it with fearful thoughts, and it becomes stronger.

Over the course of several months, as Mary's anxiety became more pervasive and the panic attacks more frequent, she began avoiding places she associated with the terrifying symptoms. As her world grew smaller, her negative anticipation became more and more exaggerated. She was caught in a vicious circle. It was at this point that we met and she began her journey to recovery.

The Answer Is *E*

After I finish taking my clients' histories, I usually ask them to tell me why they think their symptoms first appeared and why the symptoms continue to be a problem. Mary, Robert, and Kimberly gave typical responses.

> *Mary:* I have panic disorder and low self-esteem and can't seem to manage my life well.

> *Robert:* I really don't know why this [his gagging response and anxiety produced by eating] is happening. I think a childhood experience I was told about triggered all of this. My mom told me that when I was two

I swallowed a paper clip and they had to hold me upside down and that I almost choked to death. I really never thought much about it but I guess that's what triggered all of this.

Kimberly: Well I know I was assaulted and have posttraumatic stress disorder. But, I don't really know why I can't handle things better. I'm usually a very strong person.

Notice that each of the above explanations is fairly vague. In Mary's case, she uses an accurate clinical label, "panic disorder," and a pop psychology term, "low self-esteem." Terms like *panic disorder* and *posttraumatic stress disorder* are part of our modern classification system for mental health–related problems. They are essential in clinical diagnosis and research. However, these terms do nothing in themselves to help a person suffering from them understand what causes these conditions or why they continue to be a problem. Unfortunately, the substitution of a *label* or *name* for a true understanding of the *dynamics* of a process or phenomenon is very common.

Using technical labels or popular terms to describe yourself also increases the perception that you are seriously damaged and different from everyone else. One of the tasks that needs to be accomplished in order to achieve long-term recovery is to stop identifying yourself with a disorder and to see yourself as a normal person struggling with a particular problem. You are no different from anyone who has experienced a major disease or accident and has successfully returned to a normal life. Yours is simply one of the many possible struggles that humans face.

Another error people make is looking for one cause to explain everything. I often tell clients that with human beings, the answer is usually *E*, which in the multiple-choice tests you took in school usually meant "all of the above." You will see that with Mary and Robert, there was no single cause for their struggle with anxiety. Instead, there were several different factors that triggered their initial symptoms and caused those symptoms to continue to be a problem.

The idea that most anxiety-related problems are caused by several factors interacting at the same time is easy to understand. However, because we live in a culture that demands simple answers to complex problems, and are exposed to self-help books that try to give simple answers to complex problems, it often takes clients a long time to accept this.

Robert's initial explanation—a childhood trauma caused all of his symptoms—typifies one way that people search for a single cause. While factors from childhood usually do have some role in the development and maintenance of anxiety-related problems, there is rarely a single event or factor that is the primary cause. Another common form of the "one shoe fits all" approach is the idea that anxiety-related problems are due to a "chemical imbalance." The view that biology is the *only* cause of the problem is very attractive because it offers the hope that the right medication will adjust the imbalance and everything will be fine. While biology, like childhood experiences, often *does* play an important role, it is usually not the *only* cause of an anxiety-related problem. Let's now look at five factors that can combine in various ways to trigger the initial episode of frightening symptoms.

Five Factors That Can Trigger Symptoms

In chapter 2 you learned that Mary's first panic attack occurred when she was traveling and had to fly in an airplane during a storm. To her, it seemed as if the panic attack just "struck out of the blue." Several things, however, laid the foundation for this reaction. There are actually five different factors that can interact in various combinations with the beliefs and emotional baggage from childhood to trigger a person's initial panic attack. Let's look at each one individually.

Sensitive Body

Like many people with anxiety-related problems, Mary is sensitive to noise, odors, and a host of things that don't bother the average person. For example, she finds it difficult to go to sleep at her normal bedtime if she has had a cup of coffee after 4 P.M. To understand this sensitivity more fully, consider what you would find if you measured the height of a large number of people. A few would be very tall, a few would be very short, but most would be somewhere near the average. The bell-shaped curve that results from graphing this information is known as a *normal curve* and is shown on page 71.

If you measured just about any characteristic of humans—bone thickness, blood chemistry, weight—the results would be a normal curve. The sensitivity of the nervous system of people varies in this same way. A person with a sensitive body also often has greater "intuition," and tends to notice all sorts of things about situations and has a greater ability to empathize. In fact, this sensitive,

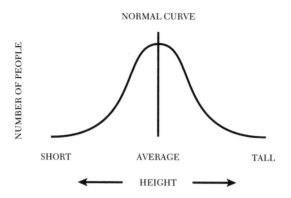

NORMAL CURVE

NUMBER OF PEOPLE

SHORT   AVERAGE   TALL

HEIGHT

empathetic, and intuitive ability is often one of the most appealing and desirable qualities a person can have. All of these qualities are simply the result of having a body that is more reactive than the average body and thus able to take in more information than the body of an average person. Unfortunately, a sensitive body also can be overloaded more easily.

Another factor that can complicate the picture for women is the actions of their hormones. Many women I work with report that their anxiety symptoms are often worse during their premenstrual period. This does *not* mean that the changes in their hormones are *causing* their symptoms, only that this additional stressor has combined with a sensitive body, weakened by the effects of prolonged anxiety, to make it easier to trip the fight-or-flight response.

The connection between a woman's hormones and anxiety is seen also in the fact that for some women, anxiety-related problems first begin right after the birth of a baby. During this time, a woman's body is still recovering from the intense effort of nurturing the unborn baby and giving birth. The hormones involved in helping a woman's body do this work are still in the process of returning to their normal levels. All of this temporarily produces an increased sensitivity. If enough of the other factors are present to produce the onset of symptoms, the panic-anxiety cycle can develop.

Medical Conditions

Because a host of medical conditions can cause anxiety and panic, the first step in working with any anxiety-related problem is to rule out physical causes through a complete examination by a physician. Examples of medical conditions associated with anxiety include cardiovascular problems, asthma, seizure disorder, diabetes, hypothyroidism, and problems with the inner ear.

In addition, many other medical conditions can make symptoms worse. One common example I frequently run into is a condition called mitral valve prolapse, or MVP, a minor defect in the heart valve that is found in 5 to 15 percent of the population. Normally, no medical treatment is required, and 50 percent of the people with this condition experience no symptoms. For the other half, the main symptom is palpitations, either in the form of premature contractions of the heart or rapid heartbeat. Other symptoms are breathlessness and vague chest pains.

Mary had MVP but had never noticed any MVP symptoms prior to the onset of her panic attacks. However, after her panic attacks developed, she began to notice some of the symptoms commonly associated with MVP. Since Mary was born with this condition, these were probably not new symptoms. After she began to pay close attention to her body, she began to notice these vague but odd sensations and they often triggered thoughts of having a heart attack or panic attack.

Drug Reaction

A wide array of medications such as stimulants, thyroid supplements, cold medications, tranquilizers, sleeping pills, certain blood pressure medications, steroids, and, ironically, antidepressants can cause anxiety symptoms. Sometimes, anxiety symptoms are due to unsupervised experimentation with or withdrawal from medications. Finally, the common legal and illegal recreational drugs, such as caffeine, alcohol, marijuana, amphetamines, and cocaine, provide yet another potential source of anxiety symptoms.

Caffeine is particularly important since it is often overlooked as a possible problem. Caffeine is a stimulant and, in fact, is the world's most widely used mood-altering drug. Even if you were able to drink coffee without any difficulty prior to the development of your anxiety-related problems, I recommend that you eliminate caffeine from your diet while you are working through this book. When you are having a problem with anxiety, it just doesn't make sense to put anything into your body that can increase anxiety. Also, be sure to check the labels of over-the-counter medications to see if they contain caffeine.

Many people find once they have achieved long-term recovery, they can resume drinking moderate amounts of caffeinated drinks without experiencing negative side effects. Others realize that they are caffeine sensitive and that it is best to avoid the drug altogether.

Hyperventilation

Hyperventilation means you are breathing (*ventilate,* to make air movement) more rapidly or deeply (*hyper,* excessively) than is necessary. When you hyperventilate, you set off a host of chemical changes in the blood because you are exhaling more carbon dioxide than normal. This can produce one or more of the following symptoms in less than a minute:

- Heart palpitations, tachycardia (racing heart), heartburn, or chest pain

- Numbness or tingling of the mouth, hands, or feet
- Dizziness, faintness, light-headedness, poor concentration, blurred vision, or a sense of separateness from the body (depersonalization)
- Shortness of breath, asthma, or a choking sensation
- Difficulty swallowing, a lump in the throat, stomach pain, or nausea
- Tension, muscle pains, shaking, or muscle spasms
- Sweating, anxiety, fatigue, weakness, poor sleep, or nightmares

When any of the above symptoms is described by a person without any of the common physical problems that might account for them, I usually find that hyperventilation is playing a major role.

Stress

Stress due to work, school, or relationship problems, or to some unusual life event, whether positive or negative, usually plays an important role in the onset of severe anxiety. At first, many of the people I work with don't realize this and tend to ignore or give very low priority to any indication that they are tired, ill, or hurt. Often, they are aware of fatigue only when it reaches the point of exhaustion. Indeed, developing effective stress management skills is often one of the keys to long-term recovery. Much more is said about stress in later chapters.

Mary's, Robert's, and Kimberly's Simple Explanations

After their first session, Mary, Robert, and Kimberly each developed simple explanations that had three parts:

1. A statement about the factors from childhood that played an important role in the development and maintenance of the problem symptoms.
2. A statement that described how the initial symptoms developed.
3. A statement that described the forces that cause the symptoms to continue to be a problem.

As you read each explanation, keep in mind that it is meant to summarize the key components that cause and maintain anxiety-related problems. Just as Mary, Robert, and Kimberly gained a deeper understanding of these shorthand explanations over time, you will find new layers of meaning for the explanation you develop as you work through the book.

Mary's Simple Explanation

Childhood Factors:

> I grew up in a home where I came to believe the lie that I was stupid and couldn't do anything right. Watching my mother, who was an alcoholic, I also came to believe that the world was dangerous and too

much for me to handle. Because all of the adults in my environment were severely damaged, I came to associate intimacy with pain and learned to ignore my own needs. When I was troubled about something, I followed the family rule: "Don't look, don't feel, run away." My mother ran away in alcohol, my father ran away in work, and I ran away in fantasy and sports.

Factors That Caused the Initial Symptoms:

My symptoms started during what I now realize was a very stressful trip. I have a reactive body and had been pushing myself. The storm caused me to worry about the plane crashing and my dying. In fact, I had worked myself up quite a bit by the time we took off. I now recall that I was also coming down with a cold. My initial symptoms were primarily due to a combination of severe hyperventilation, being sick, the storm that triggered childhood fears, and exhaustion from a tiring trip.

Factors That Maintain the Symptoms:

Because I didn't understand what had happened, and the doctor I went to see couldn't give me a reasonable explanation, I began to worry. I feared that I had some undiagnosed illness or that I might be mentally disturbed in some manner. I began to monitor my body, and whenever I noticed anything that didn't seem right, I told myself lies ("Something's wrong," "I can't handle this," etc.) and ran for safety.

Robert's Simple Explanation

Childhood Factors:

I was raised in a terribly abusive family where I developed a very poor self-image and came to believe that people always let you down. I also came to associate conflict with danger. I also have a very sensitive body that just doesn't take stress well.

Factors That Caused the Initial Symptoms:

My initial symptoms developed during the time when I had just met my current wife and was still having problems with my first wife. I was very sick when the initial choking episode occurred and had just completed a very stressful supervisor training for work. Even though I now realize that I was not in any real danger, my initial thought at that time was that I was dying. I was even thinking that if no one comes to my aid, I might not make it.

Factors That Maintain the Symptoms:

I tend to be a worrier like my mom. After the choking incident, the thought that people die from having food caught in their throats began to enter my mind whenever I was in a restaurant. I began to see myself choking to death. After awhile, just going into a restaurant would make me nervous. As I noticed the anxiety, it would trigger the fearful thoughts. Sometimes, I would become obsessed with a tickling sensation in my throat and would worry, thinking that something was caught there and that it might cause me to choke to death. Essentially, I was telling myself lies about choking, and believing them. This became a conditioned response triggered by being in restaurants or thinking about eating.

Kimberly's Simple Explanation

Childhood Factors:

I grew up in a very competitive family where I learned that I need to be strong and never show weakness, that second place means nothing, and that perfection is all that counts—all mistakes are unacceptable.

Factors That Caused the Initial Symptoms:

I experienced a terrifying assault where I was helpless and unable to protect myself. The event was so intense that my mind simply could not handle the entire picture all at once. In essence, my flashbacks have been little "snapshots" of the event that my mind has been using to process it one piece at a time. In addition, the anxiety that is triggered by things associated with the assault is simply a conditioned response. I will desensitize as I learn to accept these responses.

Factors That Maintain the Symptoms:

> I have made my symptoms worse by telling myself lies about who I am and my reaction to this event ("I'm being weak," "This shouldn't bother me so much," etc.). The truth is that these symptoms are *normal* and will lessen as time goes by. I am a *normal person* who has been in an *abnormal situation*. Part of what has driven this negative view of myself are my childhood beliefs about needing to be strong and never showing weakness. The belief that I could handle anything has also been severely shaken.

Notice how the above experiences are all simply variations on the many different types of sad experiences people face. Mary's, Robert's, and Kimberly's anxiety disorders were the normal human reactions of individuals caught in circumstances they didn't understand and that were beyond their control.

Summary of Key Ideas

1. People with anxiety-related problems often spend a great deal of time puzzling over why their problem exists.
2. Having a sound and reasonable explanation for how your anxiety-related problem developed and is maintained helps you focus your attention on what you need to do to reach long-term recovery.
3. Body scanning (also called internalization) plays a major role in maintaining symptoms. Noticing sensations that have become

associated with panic attacks and identifying them as signs of danger can trigger self-generated panic attacks.

4. The answer is *E:* Most anxiety-related problems are caused and maintained by a combination of factors. A search for a single answer is usually doomed to failure.

5. People often substitute a name or label like *panic disorder* or *low self-esteem* for true understanding of their condition. In addition to keeping a person confused, these types of labels increase the perception that you are seriously damaged and different from everyone else.

6. Five factors that can interact to generate panic disorder are a sensitive body, medical conditions, drug reactions, hyperventilation, and stress.

7. When writing a simple explanation, be sure to include the following three areas: childhood factors, factors that caused the initial symptoms, and factors that maintain the symptoms.

Recommended Activities

Continue Keeping a Journal

In the recommended activities for chapter 3 you were asked to begin keeping a journal. If you haven't already started this, I strongly urge you to do so now. Use your journal to develop your simple explanation. Record any thoughts you have about your past and the events that were taking place when your symptoms began. Include your genogram and descriptions of your childhood background. It's also a good idea to record any insights or thoughts you have concerning the work you're doing. Your journal will be a useful tool as you work through the rest of this book.

As I mentioned in chapter 3, remember that privacy is essential for journal keeping. When you keep your writing private, you're more likely to write with honesty and openness. When working with issues that have a childhood component, it is easy to forget key factors that are triggering problems. Having a place where your insights are recorded provides you a means for reviewing and reinforcing them periodically so they can become a permanent part of how you evaluate events.

When you are confident that you have fully internalized all of the learning required for long-term recovery, you may decide to destroy your journal, or you may want to keep it as a source of encouragement for the progress it records.

Write a Simple Explanation

It is now time for you to develop your own simple explanation. Follow the examples and be sure to include written statements describing the factors from childhood that played an important role in the development and maintenance of the problem symptoms; how the initial symptoms developed—be sure to list all of the sources of stress that were occurring as well as childhood factors that may have played a role; and the forces that cause the symptoms to continue to be a problem.

Take your time in developing this explanation. It may help to review the family background and childhood associations given for Mary, Robert, and Kimberly in chapters 2 and 4 and compare them with the explanations they developed. You will see that all three thought of new factors that they hadn't realized were important when they first described their backgrounds and symptoms to me. Like them, you will also experience new insights about yourself and your background as you develop your own explanation.

In developing your simple explanation, be sure to avoid the use of technical jargon. Try to state your ideas in plain everyday English. If it is difficult for you to give a clear and simple explanation, you probably haven't yet gained a good understanding of why your symptoms developed and why they continue to be a problem.

If you find it difficult to develop your simple explanation, review the previous chapters and ask someone you know and trust to help you. If you are in therapy, ask your therapist for help. If you are in a self-help group, ask the group for help. Use the explanations that Mary, Robert, and Kimberly developed as models. Four additional examples of simple explanations from other clients are given below.

The Simple Explanation of a Client with a Fear of Hospitals

Childhood Factors: As a child, I had lots of scary experiences connected with doctors due to my asthma. I also didn't think too well of myself because my parents were always criticizing me.

Factors That Caused the Initial Symptoms: When I smoked some marijuana, I had a terrifying drug reaction during which I believed I was dying. When I went to the emergency room, the staff was very critical of me when I told them I had taken cocaine. Some of what they said scared me very much. This reactivated many of my childhood fears and caused a conditioned response to things connected with hospitals and doctors.

Factors That Maintain the Symptoms: Whenever I'm in a medical setting and begin to get anxious, I tell myself the following *lies:* "The anxiety symptoms mean that I've damaged my body beyond repair. I

---

can't control what's going on. I'm helpless. The doctors are going to be able to see how stupid I was in trying that drug, and they will think badly of me." None of this is true. In fact, the exact opposite of each is reality.

The Simple Explanation of a Client with Social Phobia and Panic Disorder

Childhood Factors: I have a very sensitive body and was always shy and timid as a child. Because I didn't have many friends or do much socially as a child, I didn't gain the social skills that most people have.

Factors That Caused the Initial Symptoms: In the seventh grade I was very worried about my changing body and awkwardness. I thought I was ugly and stupid and that everybody thought poorly of me. While in English class I was supposed to give an oral book report. I became so nervous I began to shake. Thinking that everyone was laughing at me (even though they weren't), I ran from the room and soon began to hyperventilate. The symptoms were very frightening, and from that day on I began to fear that I was going crazy.

Factors That Maintain the Symptoms: For years I've told myself things that are not true. I've also become an expert at noticing any funny sensation that occurs in my body. Whenever I notice something that I've labeled as abnormal, I tell myself the following: "I'm going to have an attack and it will be terrible. People will notice my anxiety and think that I'm 'weird.' " It is these types of fearful thoughts that produce my anxiety and panic.

The Simple Explanation of a Client with Panic Disorder

Childhood Factors: I was raised in a large family where I got lost in the shuffle. I was abused when I was young, both physically and verbally. Because of this I developed the beliefs that I was tainted, broken, and somehow substandard. I also have a body that has an inherited genetic weakness (irritable bowel syndrome). The way I learned to deal with problems was to apply the rule "Don't look, don't feel, run away."

Factors That Caused the Initial Symptoms: As a young adult I developed physical symptoms due to my sensitive body and the stress of dealing with death (the deaths of three people close to me in one year). My initial symptoms were a normal reaction to stress where I hyperventilated because of real-life events that were difficult to face.

Factors That Maintain the Symptoms: Because I didn't understand what was happening and didn't want to deal with the emotional issues at hand, I created a boogeyman. Whenever I noticed any unusual sensation, I told myself lies ("I'm dying," "I can't breathe," etc.) and ran from the boogeyman.

The Simple Explanation of a Client with Panic Disorder

Childhood Factors: I grew up in a home with a controlling father and a very nonassertive and passive mother. I learned that conflict was to be avoided, and it was important to hide feelings, be compliant, and maintain the façade of being the perfect child. The message from my father was I didn't measure up unless I did things his way. I learned it was dangerous to take risks or give opinions.

Factors That Caused the Initial Symptoms: My marriage was a "dominant male, passive female" one where we presented the façade of the happy couple through the childbearing years, then divorced. I suffered a massive stress reaction after becoming a single parent; working part-time and going to paralegal school; moving back to California; working full-time; failing to receive support payments from my ex-husband; finding out that my father used inappropriate behavior toward all male children in my family, including my son, two nephews, and earlier my brother and my cousin; helping to care for three sick family members who died within six weeks of each other; suffering the loss of two close friends who moved away; having my son move back, take drugs, and be abusive; seeing my daughter run away; and finally, getting a demotion in job responsibilities at work.

Factors That Maintain the Symptoms: Because I had been trained not to deal with things directly and needed to maintain the façade of being in control, I suppressed feelings, focused on my symptoms instead of the life issues, and developed panic attacks and severe anxiety.

6

Basic Symptom-Management Skills

This chapter presents the four basic symptom-management skills Mary, Robert, and Kimberly learned during their first and second sessions.

- cue-controlled relaxation-response training
- relaxed diaphragmatic breathing
- coping self-statements
- distraction/externalization

As with most of my clients, Mary, Robert, and Kimberly each knew a little about some of these skills. Mary had practiced meditation. Robert had been told he was hyperventilating but was taking deep breaths to try to control it. Each of them was using crude forms of coping self-statements in a sporadic and ineffective manner. By going through the skills in detail, Mary, Robert, and Kimberly gained their first real tools for managing their symptoms. As you work through this chapter, be sure to take your time so you can develop the ability to apply each skill to your situation effectively.

Cue-Controlled Relaxation Response

Coined by Herbert Benson, the term *relaxation response* describes a state of deep-muscle relaxation triggered by some set method. There are many different methods that can be used to trigger a relaxation response: Progressive relaxation, biofeedback, self-hypnosis, and meditation are several. When the relaxation response is associated with a cue, such as a simple physical gesture, a word, or a mental image, it becomes a *cue-controlled relaxation response.*

One of the key features of anxiety-related problems is the association of normal, everyday activities and situations with danger. This association triggers an automatic anxiety response whenever a person does the activity or is in the situation. In theory, a person who has developed a cue-controlled relaxation response can trigger it whenever an anxiety response is experienced and neutralize that anxiety response.

In actual practice, most of the people I've seen have very strong anxiety responses that have been reinforced for several months or years. At first the cue-controlled relaxation response is weak because it is a newly conditioned response. When it is triggered in anxiety-producing situations, it may reduce anxiety only slightly. However, this small reduction, when added to the calming effect of the other tools, usually helps a person keep anxiety at a manageable level. With practice and time, the cue-controlled relaxation response becomes a stronger and more effective tool. Several different methods you can use to develop a cue-controlled relaxation response are given in appendix 4.

I routinely give all of my clients a tape at the end of the first session that helps them develop this response. This tape uses a standard procedure called progressive relaxation. It suggests that placing one of the first two fingers and thumb of either hand together will trigger similar relaxation. The pairing of the experience of relaxation with this suggestion and the actual placing of the fingers and thumb together during the exercise creates a simple conditioned response. I use the "fingers and thumb" cue because it is easy to do in most situations and is something others don't notice. (Some people use a word or image in place of the physical cue.) See the "Supplemental Materials" section for information on these tapes.

Relaxed Diaphragmatic Breathing

Chapter 5 lists the common symptoms caused by hyperventilation and describes hyperventilation as breathing more rapidly or deeply than is necessary for a given situation. It is often the result of excessive upper-chest breathing, mouth breathing because of medical or physical problems, or breath holding.

In order to understand upper-chest breathing, take a moment and lie down. Place one hand on your chest and one hand just *above* your navel. Take two or three breaths that are slightly deeper than normal and see which hand moves. If the hand on your chest moves, you are using upper-chest breathing. If the hand just above your navel moves, you are breathing with your diaphragm.

Keep in mind that both of these forms of breathing are normal. Upper-chest breathing is normal when you are exercising or excited. It is designed to help your body get plenty of oxygen. The body uses diaphragmatic breathing when there is little demand for activity. Unfortunately, many people, like Robert, use upper-chest breathing as their *primary* method of breathing, even when they are sitting or relaxed. Although it is unclear why some people become habitual upper-chest breathers, it may simply be that people who continually feel threatened by common, everyday situations trigger this breathing pattern via the activation of the fight-or-flight response.

Another explanation may stem from our culture's obsession with thin bodies and flat stomachs. Some people, particularly appearance-conscious adolescents, consciously "suck in" their stomachs in order to conform to this cultural image. This results in the habitual, unconscious tensing of the abdominal muscles. Since you cannot tense your abdomen and use diaphragmatic breathing at the same time, the body begins to use upper-chest breathing as its primary breathing pattern. Wearing tight-fitting clothes that restrict the movement of the diaphragm can also contribute to upper-chest breathing. Whatever the cause, Robert had become a habitual upper-chest breather and was thus constantly hyperventilating.

In addition to being an upper-chest breather, Robert also held his breath whenever he was in a tense situation or dealing with strong emotions. When he resumed breathing, he would either sigh or yawn, which caused a slight tingling sensation to flow down his body, the result of the momentary change in the balance of oxygen and carbon dioxide in his bloodstream—a normal response. However, because this sensation had become so associated with the severe hyperventilation he had been experiencing, Robert would notice the tingling, see it as the onset of a panic attack, and begin the negative self-talk that intensified his anxiety.

Breath holding like Robert's is a simple conditioned response that usually is learned in childhood. If someone yells at you or hits you, the natural tendency is to hold your breath. Robert's parents were constantly yelling at him. His father periodically hit him.

Because of this, any type of conflict in adulthood "felt" like danger and caused Robert to hold his breath.

There are two ways in which hyperventilation symptoms can be reduced. The first is known as the *paper bag technique.* Carry a paper bag with you and breathe into it whenever you experience the symptoms of severe hyperventilation. Since your breathing is regulated by carbon dioxide, the rapid increase of carbon dioxide in the bag as the oxygen is used up slows your breathing. If a paper bag is not handy, cup your hands over your mouth and nose and breathe into them. The paper bag technique works, but it is awkward and can be embarrassing to use in public.

Relaxed diaphragmatic breathing is a better technique. Details on how to develop this ability are given in the "Recommended Activities" section at the end of this chapter. The advantage of using relaxed diaphragmatic breathing instead of the paper bag technique is that you can use it anywhere without others knowing. If you use it at the first signs of anxiety, it is a great way to *prevent* hyperventilation from becoming severe.

Coping Self-Statements

Coping self-statements are statements you say or think to yourself that help you cope with a difficult situation. Chapter 5 listed examples of Mary's negative self-talk when she became anxious. The negative self-talk of people with anxiety-related problems usually centers around the following misconceptions:

- Something dangerous is happening to me. These symptoms are a sign of some severe mental or physical problem.
- I won't be able to function because of these symptoms.

- These symptoms will cause me to do something embarrassing.
- People will notice my problem and think I'm odd.

Developing a set of coping self-statements that challenge these misconceptions is important. Let's consider each of the above fears separately.

"These Symptoms Are a Sign of Danger"

As mentioned in chapter 5, the first step in working with any anxiety-related problem is to rule out possible "medical" causes through a complete physical examination. My clients usually do this before they see me. This means that the unpleasant symptoms they are experiencing are a combination of normal physiological processes and a conditioned response. Unfortunately, the hardest thing for people with anxiety-related problems to do is convince themselves that there is no danger in their symptoms. Indeed, one of the keys to long-term recovery is the conviction that your symptoms are harmless.

"I Won't Be Able to Function Because of These Symptoms"

Mary, Robert, and Kimberly all had many well-developed images of being incapacitated by their anxiety. By recalling these frightening images over and over, they became a reality. I find it very useful to point out to clients that by the time they see me, they have already experienced the worst episodes of anxiety they will experience. While they may experience episodes in the future that are as intense, the most frightening and intense episodes of anxiety tend to occur early in the course of an anxiety-related problem when people have the least amount of coping skills and understanding. By the time I see them, they have developed at least some coping strategies and symptom-management skills on their own.

"These Symptoms Will Cause Me to Do Something Embarrassing"

People routinely believe that they will say something crazy or do something inappropriate. Again, the knowledge that you've already experienced your worst anxiety is often helpful to remember. Because you did not act grossly inappropriately during previous episodes of intense anxiety, you've already demonstrated that you won't do anything bizarre in the future.

"People Will Notice My Problem and Think I'm Odd"

This fear is often a reflection of childhood fears of rejection and abandonment. Mary, Robert, and Kimberly all experienced rejection from their parents. They also had beliefs about being inferior to others. Their symptoms reinforced childhood fears not only about being somehow odd and inferior, but about others rejecting them because of their inferiority.

Consider how you would respond to someone experiencing severe anxiety. You would probably be compassionate and try to help this person. Likewise, this is how most others would respond to you. Besides, most of the people I work with have become experts at presenting a good front when they're anxious.

Remember that your sensitivity means you tend to notice more than the average person. Your struggle with anxiety has also made you hypersensitive to signs of anxiety. Most of the people around you lack your sensitivity and are absorbed in their own affairs, so, even if you are one of the few who shake or display other signs of anxiety, people who notice it are probably too absorbed in their own lives to give it much thought.

Examples of Coping Self-Statements

After Mary, Robert, and Kimberly developed a set of coping self-statements, they wrote them on an index card and carried them wherever they went. Since all of them tended to forget their coping self-statements during times of excessive anxiety, the cards became a tool they could use to remind themselves of the truth of their situation. Here are the cards they created:

• MARY'S CARD •

Anxiety is not dangerous; it's just uncomfortable.

I can be anxious and still function effectively.

Don't forget to trigger the relaxation response and take *relaxed* diaphragmatic breaths. They calm me.

There is nothing wrong with me. These sensations are just a conditioned response.

I've always been able to manage my anxiety and act normal in the past, even when experiencing my worst episodes. I will be able to manage it now.

People are so absorbed in their own lives that they aren't really concerned with what I'm experiencing. Even if they did

---

notice that I'm anxious, they've got other things to think about.

• ROBERT'S CARD •

I am safe; my anxiety is not dangerous.

The anxiety I'm experiencing is just a conditioned response that is being intensified because of the job stress I'm under and the lies I've been telling myself.

The original choking incident was an *unusual* situation. I have told myself lies about what it meant and my symptoms continued because I began to watch my body and repeat the old lies to myself.

This tickling in the throat and occasional cough is just a type of conditioned response. It will lessen as I desensitize myself.

My body is designed to eat. I've been eating all of my life.

Stay focused on the truth, use diaphragmatic breathing, and distract yourself.

• KIMBERLY'S CARD •

The flashbacks I'm experiencing are simply "snapshots" of the assault that my mind is using to process the trauma.

I am a *normal* person who was in an *abnormal* situation

> The anxiety I occasionally experience over things connected with the assault is a simple conditioned-response danger signal. There is no longer any danger.
>
> These symptoms won't hurt me and will lessen with time.

Externalization/Distraction

In the last chapter you learned that one of the key components to the anxiety/panic cycle is an excessive focus on the body. One of the ways to break this cycle is to shift your focus away from symptoms and onto something positive or neutral. Since focus on the body is a form of internalization, the best form of distraction is *externalization,* the focus of awareness on something outside the body. Externalization is a form of distraction, the process of shifting or diverting your attention from one activity to another, and is sometimes called *redirection.*

There are many different simple forms of externalization. Many people find it useful to focus on their surroundings when they are anxious. Mary, for example, would fix her attention on the design of a nearby wall or the clothing of people around her. Robert found that listening attentively to random conversations worked well for him. Kimberly tried a tactile approach, carrying gum with her and feeling the texture of the gum wrapper. She also liked to feel the texture of her clothes or the steering wheel of her car.

Kimberly also found it helpful, when practical, to change her immediate surroundings. For example, if she was inside, she would go outside; if she was sitting, she would stand up; if she was in the living room, she would go into the kitchen.

Simple mental activities that require concentration can also be an effective means of externalizing. When Robert became anxious, he thought of things at work or home that needed to be done and planned them out in detail. Mary, who liked to sing, found it helpful to sing when alone or, when around people, to recall the words to a song. These are more complex forms of externalization and can be difficult to do when you are very anxious, but with practice, and when used at the first signs of anxiety, they can be very effective.

Mary, Robert, and Kimberly also found they experienced fewer symptoms when they were busy with actual work. Work provides a means of distraction and keeps you focused outside of your body. When Kimberly became anxious at home, she discovered that washing dishes or cleaning something helped. Most people find work that involves some kind of physical activity, even if just with the hands, is better than purely mental activity.

Mary, Robert, and Kimberly each found that conversation provided an effective means of distraction. With Mary and Robert, only conversations with someone they knew were useful, while Kimberly found that even light banter with strangers was an effective distraction.

Externalization is more effective if you first stop and tell yourself the truth about your symptoms using your coping self-statements. An Irish adage says, "If you run from a ghost it will keep chasing you, but if you run toward it, it will disappear." When you've been telling yourself lies about anxiety—"It's dangerous," "It will make me lose control"—you need to stop and challenge the lies, then state the truth. By doing this, you are "facing the ghost" of anxiety. If, when you are anxious, you immediately try to externalize, without first stating the truth, externalization becomes just another way in which you are running from the ghost.

Summary of Key Ideas

1. Four basic symptom-management skills are cue-controlled relaxation, relaxed diaphragmatic breathing, coping self-statements, and externalization (also called redirection).
2. Many of the unpleasant symptoms associated with panic are due to hyperventilation. While the paper bag technique can reduce these symptoms, relaxed diaphragmatic breathing works better, especially when used during the early stages of anxiety.
3. Four key ideas to include in coping self-statements are "Anxiety is not dangerous," "I can experience anxiety and still function effectively," "Most people are not sensitive like me and so won't notice my symptoms," and "Most people are so busy with their own lives that, even if they notice anything, they won't care about what I'm experiencing."
4. It's useful to write several coping self-statements on index cards and memorize them. You can also carry them with you and use them to remind yourself of the truth when you are anxious.
5. The best form of distraction is externalization, focusing on something outside of your body.
6. Distraction works best if you first stop and tell yourself the truth about your symptoms with your coping self-statements.

Recommended Activities

Begin Developing Cue-Controlled Relaxation

Appendix 4 outlines several standard procedures for developing a relaxation response. As you use them, place the first two fingers and thumb of either hand together. This will associate this simple physical act with your relaxation response. This cue usually takes several practice sessions to become associated with the relaxation response and begins to become a helpful skill.

Learn Relaxed Diaphragmatic Breathing

Each night before you go to sleep, spend one to two minutes doing the following:

1. Lie flat on your back and place one hand on your chest and the other a little above your navel.
2. Close your eyes and imagine the air going all the way down to your navel.

Your goal is to breathe so that your lower hand moves up and down *gently* in a relaxed manner. Your chest may also move a little, but most of the movement should be from the diaphragm. The goal is to take small, relaxed breaths rather than big breaths. As you practice, notice that there is a slight pause just after your exhalation and before your inhalation (inhalation, exhalation, pause, inhalation, exhalation, pause). Depending on your body, this pause can last from one to several seconds. Breathing with this gentle, unforced pause is called relaxed pause breathing.

Continue practicing diaphragmatic breathing until you can (1) tell whether you're using upper-chest or diaphragmatic breathing without placing your hands on your chest and abdomen and (2) can easily take relaxed diaphragmatic breaths.

While the majority of people I work with find diaphragmatic breathing easy to learn, Robert at first found it difficult. If you experience some difficulty, try sucking in the abdominal region as you exhale. Then simply relax and do nothing as you inhale. Your abdominal region will naturally expand outward on its own. Remember, however, that your goal is to exert very little effort or attention in order to breathe diaphragmatically.

Your body already knows how to breathe diaphragmatically naturally—you use diaphragmatic breathing each night when you are in deep sleep—so you are not learning anything new. You are only developing the ability to trigger something that your body already does. Once Robert understood this, he quickly mastered the ability to breathe diaphragmatically.

One commonly mistaken idea about breathing is that you should take a deep breath when you are anxious. When I first discussed diaphragmatic breathing with Mary, she reported that she already knew how to do it. However, since she was continuing to experience much light-headedness and a "lack of air," it was evident that hyperventilation was still a problem. When I asked her to show me what she was doing, she took several very large diaphragmatic breaths.

Taking large diaphragmatic breaths, like rapid upper-chest breathing, increases hyperventilation symptoms. So, while Mary could easily take diaphragmatic breaths, she was using this ability in a way that increased rather than decreased her symptoms. The key to using diaphragmatic breathing is to take relaxed breaths that are similar to those you take when resting. Within a week

Mary had mastered this skill and it greatly reduced the amount of hyperventilation symptoms she experienced.

While diaphragmatic breathing is a powerful skill, it is important to avoid becoming overly concerned with your breathing. Keep your practice sessions short, just one or two minutes. Do not make this hard work. You have been breathing all of your life and, as has already been mentioned, your body already knows how to take relaxed diaphragmatic breaths. You are merely learning how to do it consciously. If you experience a sense of light-headedness or one of the other hyperventilation symptoms, you are working too hard at the exercise. Take smaller and more relaxed breaths.

After you have mastered diaphragmatic breathing while lying down, practice two or three times a day while standing or sitting. You'll probably find it to be more difficult at first, but with practice, you will find breathing with your diaphragm to be easy and your normal method of breathing, even if you are a habitual upper-chest breather like Robert.

Once you learn how to use this skill, take three or four slow, relaxed diaphragmatic breaths at the first signs of anxiety.

Create Several Coping Self-Statements

Create four to six coping self-statements of your own and write them on an index card you can carry with you. Begin to refer to them whenever you experience anxiety. If you like any of those created by Mary, Robert, or Kimberly, use them exactly as written or, if their statements do not fit your personality or life situation, change the wording to compose new ones that do apply. It is important that your coping self-statements have power and meaning for you.

Create a "Summary Card"

In addition to your coping self-statement card, create a card that summarizes your basic anxiety symptoms–management skills. Here is an example of one I routinely use with clients:

• SKILLS SUMMARY CARD •

1. Use the cue that triggers your relaxation response.
2. Take three or four *relaxed* diaphragmatic breaths.
3. Read your coping self-statements.
4. Distract yourself; externalize.

7

Distorted Thinking

Within three weeks Mary, Robert, and Kimberly had all developed simple explanations for their conditions and were beginning to gain some mastery of the four basic symptom-management skills presented in the last chapter. As a result, they began to move into what, in chapter 1, is called the first level of recovery, or basic symptom control. Even though they were still having acute symptoms, they were beginning to experience their first taste of success in managing anxiety.

The next step in their treatment was to help them identify and challenge habitual thinking patterns that contributed to the development of the problem and supported the maintenance of their symptoms, and, then to show them how to change the dysfunctional behaviors that had developed because of their symptoms. This chapter focuses on the first of these two goals, while chapter 8 focuses on the second.

Distorted Thinking

The way you think is, for the most part, a habit pattern not very different from the hundreds of other habit patterns you've developed during your life. Much of your thought is characterized by conversations you have inside your head, called *self-talk*. Sometimes you are very aware of your self-talk. However, much of your self-talk is done in an automatic and habitual manner. It's as if a particular situation causes a specific habitual response that includes a prerecorded tape that plays inside your head.

Everyone has habitual ways in which they process information that distort reality. I call these types of thinking patterns *distorted thinking*. This book uses a simplified system that places the major types of distorted thinking into three groups.

- Overgeneralization
- Magnification/Minimization
- Emotional reasoning

As you read about the various forms of distorted thinking, keep in mind that *everyone* uses them regularly. In fact, if you simply pay attention to casual conversations you hear during the day, you will be able to identify many examples of these types of distorted thinking.

Overgeneralizations

Generalizations are a necessary and important part of everyday life. Everyone develops hundreds of generalizations about reality. Some common examples include:

- Vegetables are good for you.
- It's good to be punctual.
- People are usually honest.

Generalizations such as these help us deal with events without the need to think about them in detail. When a generalization is transformed into an absolute rule, it becomes an *overgeneralization*. There are three common forms of overgeneralizations: all-or-nothing thinking, should/must thinking, and circular questioning.

All-or-nothing thinking is a thought or statement characterized by words like *never, always,* and *every.* Here are a few examples:

- I can never get things right.
- I'm always late.
- This happens to me every time I try to do this.

Should/must thinking takes the form of a thought or statement characterized by words like *should, must, can't,* or *have to.* For instance, "It's good to be punctual," becomes "I should be punctual," "I must be on time," "I can't be late," or "I have to be punctual."

Although the above kinds of overgeneralization tend to be easy to spot, there is a subtle form of distorted thinking related to overgeneralization that I call *circular questioning.* Circular questioning is the act of asking a series of questions over and over without any real attempt to answer them. When you watch people using circular questioning it appears as though they have "short-circuited" in some fashion. Actually, they have only become confused because reality is not conforming to one or more of their beliefs about how the world "should" be.

Individuals suffering from anxiety-related problems often spend much time engaged in circular questioning about their condition, with thoughts or self-talk such as "Why can't I just go out and do things like others? It's so silly. I just don't understand why I make such a big deal out of everything." This type of circular questioning reflects the confusion that is generated when your body reacts in a way you believe it "shouldn't" be reacting, or you behave in a way you believe you "shouldn't" be behaving.

To achieve long-term recovery, you need to understand the forces that drive your thoughts and behavior, and redefine who you are. This is one of the reasons that the development of a simple explanation that answers these types of questions is so important. It is your first step in coming to terms with aspects of yourself of which you were previously unaware. Your simple explanation also helps you to focus on the task of using your skills to manage your symptoms.

Because circular questioning is so common, let's look at another everyday example of circular questioning that Mary engaged in when a friend disappointed her.

> I just don't understand why Barbara didn't call like she said she would. She's usually not like that. It doesn't make sense. Why would she do this when she knows how important this was to me.

As with many people, Mary believed that everyone else lived by the same types of rules she used to govern her own life. One of those rules was "you should always do what you say you're going to do." Her circular questioning was a reflection of the confusion caused by her overgeneralization of that rule when confronting the reality that Barbara did not do what she said she was going to do.

After listening to Mary's circular questioning, I responded with "Tell me why you think she did that." Like most people who are asked to provide an answer to the "whys" of circular questioning, Mary had no immediate answer. However, after a minute of thought and a little prompting she quickly began to generate numerous possibilities. Here are a few. See if you can think of others.

- Maybe something important came up.
- Maybe Barbara didn't realize how important it was.
- There might have been some sort of misunderstanding.

In addition, we could add at least two more: Some people are dishonest and make agreements all of the time that they know they have no intention of honoring. Others have unresolved issues from childhood that prevent them from following through on what they say. What a wonderful world it would be if everyone followed Mary's rule and always did what they said they were going to do. However, in the real world we frequently encounter people who do not.

Whenever you notice yourself engaged in circular questioning, remind yourself that it is simply an indication that you are having difficulty accepting the fact that some aspect of reality and your expectations are clashing. When this occurs, remind yourself that reality is often different from what you would like it to be and redirect your focus to how you should respond.

One of the keys to ending circular questioning is learning that life is a series of choices. We assess situations as best we can, then choose actions that either move us toward those things we want or protect us from harm. Applying this idea to Mary's situation, she needed to shift her focus away from "Why did Barbara do this?" to "How am I going to respond to her actions?" The next time you find yourself engaged in circular questioning, do the following.

- Answer your questions.
- Shift your focus to deciding how you are going to respond.

Here's how Mary applied this two-step approach to her circular questioning about Barbara:

Let's answer the "whys." I know Barbara is very busy and has a lot on her mind with her sick son. She probably just forgot. I also know that while calling is a big deal to me, it probably isn't as important to Barbara.

Now, let's focus on how I can respond. While I wish Barbara would be more responsible, she is the way she is and there is nothing I can do to change it. If I want to maintain the friendship, I need to accept that she's going to be thoughtless from time to time. This means I cannot depend on her to respond the way I want her to respond. If I cannot accept this, I need to find new friends who will respond in a way that meets my needs.

Magnification/Minimization

Magnification is the term used to describe the act of exaggerating or "magnifying" an event into something bigger or worse than it actually is. This is also called *catastrophizing* because a minor difficulty or problem is transformed into a catastrophe. When Robert would feel anything in his throat that seemed odd, he would magnify it into a life-threatening event. When Kimberly considered the possibility of not working at her old position because she no longer felt safe there, she magnified it into a major personal defeat. Here are some examples of catastrophic self-talk used when describing a panic attack:

- It's terrible when I get anxious.
- The feeling is absolutely awful.
- I just can't stand it.

As was mentioned in the discussion on coping self-statements, this type of self-talk increases symptoms and makes you feel worse than you otherwise would. It is important to understand that you *can stand* anxiety. Indeed, one of the goals of desensitization is to prove to yourself that you can be anxious and still function. Although anxiety can be very uncomfortable, you can learn how to manage it and return to normal activities. To say you cannot stand anxiety is to believe a lie. The fact is you have withstood it; you have survived. As mentioned previously, one of the keys to long-term recovery is learning the truth about anxiety and yourself, and accepting this truth.

Minimization is often called *discounting* and refers to when you diminish or belittle positive aspects about yourself or things connected with you. For example, when I first pointed out how much calmer Kimberly was at home and in a variety of situations outside of the home, she responded with statements like "I'm not really that much better. If I was, I'd quit getting so nervous every time I go to a mall and see someone who looks like the student who assaulted me." Kimberly's perfectionism made it difficult for her to acknowledge small improvements. For her, the only thing that counted was to have no symptoms.

Emotional Reasoning

Emotional reasoning refers to irrational thoughts that are generated by unconscious associations or negative core beliefs. These thoughts usually are accompanied by strong negative emotions. One common form of emotional reasoning is *personalization*, which can be defined as assuming responsibility for a negative event when there is no logical basis for doing so.

Kimberly presents a good example of personalization. At the beginning of our work together she would often say things such as

"I should have known that student was dangerous. I don't know how I could have been so careless." This type of self-talk is based on the assumption that Kimberly *should* always know what is going on around her and have the correct response.

In chapter 4 we identified one of Kimberly's core beliefs as "Mistakes are not acceptable." In life, we often are unaware of important things occurring around us and make choices that turn out poorly. Sometimes things happen for reasons that have nothing to do with us, as was the case with Kimberly's assault. The assault on Kimberly was a surprise to everyone. No one suspected that this particular student would behave in this manner. Still, Kimberly constantly belittled herself for not having the ability to see something that *no* reasonable human being could have seen. In essence, Kimberly was acting on the irrational assumption that she should have a godlike ability always to know what is happening around her and have the perfect response for every situation.

Mind reading is another common form of emotional reasoning, characterized by the assumption that you know what another person is thinking even though there is little evidence to support your conclusion. When Mary went to events where there were many people, she often thought, "Everyone here can see that I'm having a problem doing what is so easy for them. They all probably think it's stupid that I'm so weak." This is a common form of self-talk for people who have a poor self-image.

In chapter 4 we identified two of Mary's core beliefs as "I'm inferior to others" and "I can't do anything correctly." Furthermore, just as Mary assumed that she was able to read the minds of others, she also assumed that they were reading her mind and aware of how distressed she was. One of the ideas that Mary found liberating was the fact that most people are so wrapped up in themselves that they usually don't notice others. And if they do notice anything unusual, they usually forget about it very quickly and refocus on themselves.

Another way of countering mind reading is to consider how you would react to someone in your situation. When I asked Mary how she would respond if she saw someone who seemed anxious, she said, "My heart would go out to that person. I wouldn't think that person was stupid or inferior." *Most* people you meet will have a similar reaction. The few who would look down on you aren't the type of people you want in your life because their reaction is driven by immature or irrational thinking.

Fortune-telling, a third type of emotional reasoning, is when you make a prediction and then respond to it as if it were a fact. In Robert's case, he would often visualize himself having difficulty eating one to two hours before it was time to eat. When it actually became time to eat, he had worked himself into such a high level of anxiety that the dry mouth and other physiological responses associated with fear made it difficult for him to eat. In essence, his fears became a self-fulfilling prophecy.

A fourth type of emotional reasoning, called *accepting questionable sources as authoritative,* is the acceptance of an opinion or advice from someone whose thinking is distorted by their own personal issues, ignorance, lack of experience, or prejudice. Mary supplies a good example of this form of emotional reasoning. One of her friends from childhood, Judy, would often assess Mary's behavior as thoughtless or due to self-centeredness. As we discussed some of these situations, it became evident that Judy had a difficult time accepting responsibility for mistakes and tended to put down everyone she knew. Still, Mary tended to react to everything Judy said as if it were the absolute truth, even though most of Judy's assessments were wrong.

Her acceptance of Judy's questionable opinion as authoritative was based on Mary's core beliefs that she was inferior to others and couldn't do things correctly. The logical extension of these beliefs was that others could see things more clearly than she and therefore, must be more accurate in their assessments. In actuality, Mary was a very intelligent woman with a strong ability to evaluate people and situations. She had just never viewed herself that way. One of the keys for her long-term recovery was to begin to trust her ability to assess situations and make good judgments. She had to learn to quit minimizing her own abilities and magnifying those of others.

Challenging Irrational and Negative Self-Talk

To all outward appearances, prior to the onset of their symptoms, Mary, Robert, and Kimberly were living what seemed like normal lives. They were employed and going about their everyday activities like anyone else. On reflection, however, all three saw how this normal-looking exterior hid the fact that distorted thinking was playing a major role in their everyday lives. More importantly, distorted thinking played a subtle yet key role in the development of their anxiety-related problems and an even greater role in maintaining them.

Once the initial episodes of anxiety occur, distorted thinking tends to become even more pronounced. One of the roles it takes is to reinforce the negative beliefs and associations from childhood. Thus, Mary's childhood belief that she was inferior to others was confirmed by the fact that she now couldn't handle even simple trips outside of her town. Robert's childhood belief that something was wrong with him was confirmed by the fact that he was unable to eat anything other than baby food. Kimberly's childhood belief that mistakes were unacceptable transformed the student's unpredictable assault into a "mistake" that she had "allowed to happen," which, in turn, became a nightmare that was even worse than the assault.

To achieve long-term recovery, Mary, Robert, and Kimberly had to learn how to identify and effectively challenge the cognitive distortions that had become habits. Here is an example of a rational challenge Kimberly developed:

Kimberly's Negative Self-Talk about the Possibility of Transferring to a New Position

> I can't stand it when I think about going back to my old position. I don't know why I can't get it together and go back to the way I used to be. Instead, I keep thinking about running away to a new position.

Kimberly's Rational Challenge

> First of all, I can stand it when I think about what happened. While it still makes me very anxious, I am able to think about it, and I continue to function. I don't become comatose or paralyzed. More important, I know that the anxiety I feel when I think about going back is an important *message*. Maybe it is time I moved on. I'm different because of the assault. The fact that I'm mortal is much more real to me. I also realize that it is possible for a stronger person to overpower me. I'm not invincible. Transferring to a new position is not a sign of failure. It's simply an acknowledgment of the fact that at this stage of my life I don't want to expose myself to dangers that I used to ignore. People make choices like this all the time. It's just a reflection of

maturity and a desire to be in a less dangerous environment and nothing more.

In addition to confronting the distorted thinking you have identified, it often is useful to include a rational challenge to the core beliefs or associations that generated the negative self-talk. Here is another example demonstrating this:

Kimberly's Negative Self-Talk Concerning the Assault

I should have known this student was dangerous. I don't know how I could have been so careless.

Kimberly's Rational Challenge

Although I knew that this student, like all the others, had potential for violence, there was nothing in his chart or file that indicated he was more dangerous than the others. I took all the usual precautions that had always been sufficient in the past. The simple truth is that this person was bigger and stronger than me, and I had no help. His behavior was unpredictable and unusual. If there is any responsibility to be assigned, it is to the lack of staffing at that site. I did the best I could do in those circumstances. It simply wasn't enough. I am not God. I don't know everything that is going on and I don't always have the ability to do what I would like to do.

The thing that makes this such a big problem is my desire never to be weak. I know this comes from the constant competition with my dad and his constant put-downs whenever I made a mistake or showed weakness. He was unreasonable. Unfortunately, I've internalized him and can be unreasonable with myself. It's OK to make mistakes and be human. I certainly don't want to go through life the way he has.

Summary of Key Ideas

1. Everyone has habitual ways in which they process information that distort reality. These can be placed into three general categories: overgeneralizations, magnification/minimization, and emotional reasoning.

2. There are three common types of overgeneralizations: all-or-nothing thinking, should/must thinking, and circular questioning.

3. Magnification exaggerates an event into something bigger or worse than it actually is. Minimization or discounting refers to when you diminish or belittle positive aspects about yourself or things connected to you.

4. There are four common types of emotional reasoning: personalization, mind reading, fortune-telling, and accepting questionable sources as authoritative.

5. Most people are so wrapped up in themselves that they usually don't notice others. If they do notice anything unusual, they usually forget about it very quickly and refocus on themselves.

6. Distorted thinking plays an important role in the development of symptoms and helps to maintain symptoms by reinforcing negative beliefs and associations from childhood.

7. Learning to identify and effectively challenge distorted thinking is one of the keys to long-term recovery.

Recommended Activities

Continue Developing Skills with the "Basics"

Chapter 6 presented four basic skills for managing anxiety. If you have not yet done the exercises at the end of that chapter, do them now before you go on. If you have been working on them but feel you still are not using them effectively, take a few days to review chapter 6 and make sure you are using each skill properly.

Begin to Identify and Challenge Your Distorted Thinking

For ten or fifteen minutes each day, think about events that have upset you. These could be situations that caused anxiety, anger, or sadness. Record as much of what you were saying to yourself during these events as you can recall. After you've recorded your self-talk, identify any forms of distorted thinking that were used. If you have difficulty remembering what you were thinking, ask yourself, "Why was this situation so important to me?" This question usually triggers a host of thoughts about yourself and the situation. Write these down.

Next, write out a rational challenge to that distorted thinking. Be sure to include a challenge for any core belief or association that is implied by what you said or thought. Keep in mind that some of your thoughts will probably be rational responses. Others will reflect problems that need to be worked out. Robert recorded the following self-talk, triggered by a friend's request to go out to eat:

I can't do this. I hate it when I'm asked to do something I don't want to do. Why does this have to happen to me now? I know I'm not going to be able to handle this. I'll go and gag on something and make a complete fool of myself.

Notice that the statement "I hate it when I'm asked to do something I don't want to do" is a simple statement of fact. No challenge is required for this. Furthermore, the request from Robert's friend is a simple problem that can be stated as "Do I accept or refuse the request?" Here is Robert's rational challenge:

Boy, here I go again. I know that I'm not ready to eat in restaurants yet. If I choose to go, I can always say I'm not hungry and order a soda. I know I can drink without any problem. As for not liking these types of requests, this is just a statement of fact. I also know that my reaction is due to the fact that it reminds me of the difficulty I'm having with eating. The negative images of my gagging and being embarrassed are simple fortune-telling. I can make choices that will prevent this from happening. Part of what's driving these images are the old childhood memories of being ridiculed. I'm an adult now and these people are different from the kids who used to tease me.

Review this chapter at least two times, paying close attention to the examples. Reviewing the genogram and list of core beliefs you developed while working in chapters 2 and 4 will also help you develop stronger rational challenges.

Identify Distorted Thinking in the People You Know

A simple assignment that Mary, Robert, and Kimberly all found very useful was to spend a week identifying distorted thinking used by the people in their lives. The purpose of this assignment is twofold: First, you will gain skill in identifying common forms of distorted thinking. Second, you will see how distorted thinking is a *common* way in which people think. Keep this second point in mind as you begin to notice your own distorted thinking. *Everyone* uses distorted thinking from time to time. Having distorted thinking *does not* mean you are crazy. While the goal of this book is to help you reduce the occurrence of your distorted thinking, you will never eliminate all of it. Distorted thinking is just another *normal* aspect of being human.

During the week that you do this exercise, take a few minutes in the morning to review the various types of distorted thinking discussed in this chapter. Then, while you talk with others, watch television, listen to people talking on the radio, or listen to people talking around you, identify the various types of distorted thinking you hear. Make a game out of it, but *do not tell others what you are doing.* Many people become defensive or offended when their distorted thinking is pointed out. Here is a list of the three general types of distorted thinking discussed in this chapter along with the forms that each type takes:

    Overgeneralizations
      All-or-Nothing Thinking
      Should/Must Thinking
      Circular Questioning

Magnification/Minimization
(Also called catastrophizing and discounting)
Emotional Reasoning
Personalization
Mind Reading
Fortune-Telling
Accepting Questionable Sources as Authoritative

While some people become very skilled in labeling their various forms of distorted thinking, others find it difficult. While many people find that using the labels makes identification easier, keep in mind that your goal is to be able to *recognize* and *challenge* distorted thinking. If you achieve this goal, it doesn't matter whether or not you are able to label your distorted thinking correctly.

As you do this exercise, you may find that some of the people you know use a lot of distorted thinking. In fact, their distorted thinking may be something that causes problems in your relationships with them. If this is the case, realize that you probably won't be able to change the way they think. Instead, focus on your response to their distorted thinking. The problem of dealing with difficult people is discussed in more detail in later chapters in relation to the topics of healthy boundaries and D.E.R. scripts.

8

Progressive
Desensitization

In chapter 3 we discussed how a neutral stimulus can trigger a conditioned response and how desensitization is the process of becoming unresponsive to that stimulus. This chapter describes how to desensitize in a gradual, step-by-step manner called *progressive desensitization*. "Progressive" refers to the fact that you begin with situations that trigger the lowest levels of anxiety and slowly work up, or progress, to those situations that trigger the highest levels of anxiety.

Developing a Plan

The key to success with desensitization is having a well thought out approach that is applied in an orderly manner. Mary presents a good example of how this is done. We first made a list of those types of situations that triggered anxiety for her and rated them from 1 to 10 according to how much anxiety each one produced and how often Mary avoided the situation. The scales we used and the list Mary developed are shown below.

Level of Anxiety

0	1	2	3	4	5	6	7	8	9	10

No Anxiety · Extreme Panic

Level of Avoidance

0	1	2	3	4	5	6	7	8	9	10

No Avoidance · Avoid Approximately 50 percent of the time · Always Avoid

Mary's Problem Situations

Situation	Level of Anxiety	Level of Avoidance
Running within 4 miles of home	2	0
Running 4–10 miles from home	4–5	3
Running on the mountain near my home	8	10
Running any course more than 10 miles from home	10	10
Being in crowds with someone I know	6	8
Being in crowds by myself	8	9
Dining out with someone I know	6	6
Dining out alone	8	9
Going to the theater alone or with someone I know	8	10
Driving out of town alone or with someone I know	10	10

Once the list was developed, the next step was to select a specific goal. Progressive desensitization is most effective when the first goal is something that produces a relatively low level of anxiety and has some practical benefit. This helps to ensure success and provides you with motivation to do the sometimes tedious work involved in desensitizing yourself.

In Mary's case, she loved to run and wanted to resume running old courses that she quit using when her anxiety became too intense. Since running close to home presented no problem for her, we developed a series of routes that were progressively farther from her home. These were areas where she had run before and where she wanted to be able to run again. We labeled them Course 1, Course 2, and Course 3. The final course took her on a path that went slightly up a mountain where she used to train but which now provoked too much anxiety.

After developing specific practice goals, I had Mary close her eyes and think about running on these practice courses. I then had her describe all of the physical sensations that she feared may occur along with all of the fearful thoughts that would come up in these situations. This is what she reported:

Fearful Body Sensations
Rapid heartbeat
Sweating
Light-headedness
Faintness
Fatigue
"Gasping for air"

Fearful Thoughts
Something's wrong with me.
I'm going to faint.

I'm going to have a heart attack.
What if someone sees me like this?
What if I can't get help?
I'm going to die here all alone.

The next step was to develop a coping self-statement for each of the above frightening sensations and thoughts. Mary reworked her coping self-statement index card and came up with the following two cards. The first addressed the body sensations she feared. The second addressed her fearful thoughts.

> There is nothing wrong with me. My doctor says I'm healthy as a horse. When I run, my heart is supposed to beat fast. I'm supposed to sweat and get winded when I push hard. Afterward, I'm supposed to be fatigued. These are not signs of a problem. They are things I've experienced ever since I began to run. They are *normal* and *safe*. They are simply signs that my body is functioning the way it is supposed to function. My fears about them in the past were *lies* I believed because I didn't understand what had happened to me on the airplane flight during the storm.

> There is nothing wrong with me. I've never fainted even though I've feared this for a long time. I've simply hyperventilated and *thought* I was going to faint. Likewise, my heart is healthy.
> As far as people noticing that I'm anxious, I'm an expert at

being cool on the outside even when I'm panicked on the inside. Besides, most people are too into themselves to notice anything much about a stranger. Even if they do notice something, they usually don't pay much attention to it one way or the other.

As far as dying alone goes, this is really a stretch. However, if this were to occur, it would probably happen fast and I wouldn't be worrying about it anymore. Why worry about something that is very unlikely and over which you have no control?

Basic Guidelines for Practicing

Before beginning, you should understand the basic principles of practicing. Here is the list I give my clients:

1. Practice Regularly

The goal of practicing is twofold: First, you need to expose yourself to anxiety-producing triggers enough times so that you become desensitized and no longer react to them. Second, you are convincing yourself that you can face these fearful situations and continue to function and manage your anxiety effectively no matter how you feel. The only way to do this is through *regular* practice.

There are times when illness, work, or other problems will interfere with your practice. However, do not wait until you "feel up to it" to practice. If you had a life-threatening disease, taking medication essential for recovery would be one of your highest priorities. Practice *will* allow you to desensitize if it is done systematically and regularly. When thoughts such as "Why do I have to do this" or "This is so hard" come up, remind yourself of the benefits you will enjoy once your goal is accomplished. These include both the freedom of doing what you want and feeling better about yourself.

A good *general rule* is to practice for at least an hour three times a week, daily if possible. *You cannot practice too much.* Practice regularly, as much as you can, for as long as you can.

2. Repetition Is the Key to Success

Always practice a particular situation several times before moving on to the next goal. Just because you did it once with a low level of anxiety does not mean that you are desensitized to it. You'll want to practice a given situation several times so you will have experienced it during times when you are feeling relatively calm as well as when you are feeling anxious. Only then will you be fully convinced that you have mastered that situation and can function regardless of how anxious you are.

3. Learn to Tolerate Distress

Your goal is to convince yourself that anxiety is something you can tolerate. Remember that although extreme anxiety and panic are uncomfortable, they cannot hurt you. They will not harm your body or cause any kind of insanity. Remember that you have probably experienced the worst anxiety you will ever experience. Although it was frightening, it did not cause any physical harm.

4. Remember That Anxiety Is Normal

Anxiety always accompanies new activities, so expect some anxiety to occur whenever you start a new practice goal. Remember that some of what you are experiencing is the excitement you experience whenever you challenge yourself. In other words, you may simply be mislabeling excitement as anxiety!

5. Expect Progress to Be Three Steps Forward and One Step Backward

A simple fact of life is that on some days you feel better than on others. Sometimes this is due to unusual life events. Sometimes it is not clear why it happens. However, you will occasionally slip back into old behaviors and find that situations you thought you had conquered still trigger anxiety. This is a normal and natural part of the learning process. Often it is simply due to being tired or to the presence of several normal life stressors that happen to be occurring together.

6. Practice with as Many Factors in Your Favor as Possible

When practicing a new activity, try to keep as many factors as possible—such as time of day, size of crowd, etc.—in your favor. Once a situation is mastered with everything in your favor, you can begin practicing during times when it is more difficult.

7. Use Your Coping Skills at the First Sign of Anxiety

Do not "save" your skills for times when you are feeling panicky. Remember that they are most effective when used at the first sign of anxiety.

8. Keep Pushing Yourself a Little Bit Further

Your goal is to practice in situations that produce low-level anxiety, level 3–5 on our scale (page 121). If your anxiety has reduced to 1–2, and you have practiced a particular goal several times, advance to the next step. *Do not wait until you are completely at ease with a specific situation before you move on.*

If you are not quite ready to proceed to the next goal but find you easily accomplish a practice session, either extend the time you spend on the activity or do just a little more than you had planned. At the same time, if you are panicky, reexamine your desensitization goal and break it into smaller, easier steps.

9. Remember That Desensitization Is a Trial-and-Error Process

There is no way to know before you begin how rapidly you should proceed with your desensitization goals. Identifying the most realistic desensitization goals at any given time is the result of trial and error. You discover what is "too much" by doing too much. This will occasionally occur. When it does, it simply means that your goal needs to be broken down into two or more steps.

Examples

Usually, I like to have a client master some of the cognitive self-talk skills discussed in the last chapter before beginning desensitization. However, because Robert's symptoms were causing major interference with his daily life, we focused on basic coping strategies and began setting up desensitization goals during our second and third sessions.

Our first goal was to reduce the intensity of the panic attacks Robert was experiencing at work. Robert did not want to take medication so we decided to see what we could accomplish with the four basic skills described in chapter 6. During the first session, I always ask about a client's quality of sleep. Robert was not sleeping well. He had difficulty falling asleep and would sometimes wake up and find it difficult to get back to sleep. Whenever I hear this from a client, I immediately establish the improvement of the quality of their sleep as a goal.

Lack of sleep greatly reduces your body's ability to tolerate stress and your mind's ability to think clearly, both of which tend to increase all of the symptoms you're experiencing. If a person can sleep better, there is usually a marked improvement. The body is able to make routine repairs, providing more mental and physical resources for coping with anxiety. The first step in helping Robert improve the quality of his sleep was to go over the guidelines listed in "Recommended Activities" at the end of chapter 3 for people who are sleeping poorly. I then instructed him to keep a tape recorder next to his bed and use the relaxation-response tape when he was ready to go to sleep. (See the "Supplemental Materials" section at the end of this book for information on obtaining this tape.)

While Robert was very restricted in what he could eat, he was working with his doctor to ensure that he received proper nourishment. At the same time, he was experiencing so much anxiety at work that he was isolating himself in his office and making every excuse he could think of to avoid coming into contact with others. While no one had said anything to him yet, there was the real possibility that this could soon become an issue with his superiors. Therefore, we decided that his greatest immediate need was to reduce the symptoms he was experiencing at work. Here are the situations Robert identified as troublesome:

Robert's Problem Situations

Situation	Level of Anxiety	Level of Avoidance
Walking outside my office door 20 feet to speak with my secretary	4	3
Walking around the unit outside of my door	5	3
Walking into another unit	5	4
Walking into the production area	4	3
Going into the conference room when no one is there	6	4
Going into the conference room for a weekly meeting	8	5
Going into the conference room for a special meeting	8	5
Talking with my supervisor	8	6
Talking with the employees under me	3	1
Going into the company cafeteria	8	8
Going into the company lounge	8	10

It is important to start with realistic expectations. We quickly realized that there was no immediate need for Robert to be able to go to the cafeteria and there was no practical way to set up a progressive desensitization schedule for meetings, two situations that triggered very high levels of anxiety and panic. On the other hand, Robert was fairly comfortable speaking with employees who were not his superiors, and he could practice being in his immediate work area without being obvious about what he was doing. Therefore, we selected the following initial goals:

1. Walking outside my office to speak with my secretary (instead of using the intercom)
2. Walking outside my office to speak to my immediate subordinates (instead of having my secretary relay my instructions)
3. Walking down the hall to the conference room and sitting in it when no one is there
4. Walking into the production area

Four-Step Approach to "What Ifs"

The symptoms that Robert feared when he imagined himself doing the above were the same as those listed by Mary. One additional fearful thought that was especially strong was "What if I have a panic attack?" We addressed this fear using what I call the *four-step approach to "what ifs."*

1. How likely is it that the feared event will occur?
2. How serious would it be if this happened?
3. What steps can I take to prevent this event from taking place?
4. What can I do to cope with the event if it does happen?

Here is a summary of Robert's answers after we discussed each one at length:

How Likely Is It That I Will Have a Panic Attack?

Looking at the past few weeks, there is probably only a 25-percent chance that I'll have a full-blown panic attack in the situations I've chosen to put myself in. While I often become very anxious, I usually have major attacks only in the more stressful situations. Even though I don't like it, I can handle anxiety.

How Serious Would It Be If I Had a Panic Attack?

There are no serious consequences other than being very uncomfortable. I'm not losing any money or possessions. No physical harm is done to me or anyone I love. I'm just miserable and feeling shame and embarrassment. I'm an expert at being miserable. I've also experienced lots of shame and embarrassment. While I don't like them, I can endure them. I also know from experience that I am a real professional at appearing normal even when I'm having a panic attack.

What Steps Can I Take to Prevent a Panic Attack?

I can glance over my coping self-statements and the card that summarizes my basic skills before leaving my office. I can also choose to go out when it is less busy. Having something to eat periodically also helps.

What Can I Do to Cope with a Panic Attack?

First, I can take several relaxed diaphragmatic breaths and trigger my relaxation response. Next, I can repeat my coping self-statements. I have memorized the various explanations I could give to others, so I can leave if I feel the need.

Robert summarized the above ideas into the following coping self-statement:

> While there's the possibility that I may have a panic attack, I usually do fine in these situations. The anxiety I do experience is usually not that bad. I now have new tools for managing my symptoms and know how to get back to my safe area if I'm more uncomfortable than I want to be. I also know that there is nothing dangerous about what I'm experiencing.

Robert began taking frequent short excursions into the locations at work to which he wanted to become desensitized. He would first review his notes, then spend fifteen to forty-five minutes in a specific area. He worked through each area, one at a time, until he could again go comfortably to all of the areas in his unit. As with most people who experience anxiety-related symptoms, Robert was very creative. He was able to make his excursions look like they were part of his job so others didn't realize what he was doing.

Increased Suggestibility

People with severe anxiety often are more suggestible to negative ideas, especially those that are associated with their anxiety. This heightened suggestibility can intensify the various types of negative and catastrophic thinking discussed in this chapter and become a major force that interferes with desensitization and promotes a state of excessive anxiety.

Suggestibility is the acceptance of an idea without analyzing it critically. Suggestibility is sometimes very useful. For example, when you watch a movie, your ability to ignore the fact that you are just watching moving images and listening to recorded sounds allows you to enter into the movie as if you were actually there, experiencing what the characters were experiencing. Sometimes, though, suggestibility can be damaging, as in the case of Mary or Robert. Whenever they heard or read about problems that were sometimes associated with severe anxiety, they failed to analyze what they read carefully and, instead, would immediately believe that what they read must also be true for them. As they dwelled on what they had read, their fear would generate symptoms that seemed to confirm what they had feared.

Mary, for instance, heard that suicide was associated with panic disorder. She began to worry that she might commit suicide, and within a few days this became an overwhelming obsession. While many people with severe anxiety do have occasional suicidal thoughts, they are usually just passing ones, such as "I wish I were dead," and are similar to those that anyone experiencing major difficulties might have. I've worked with hundreds of people, and it has been very rare when a person with panic disorder has had serious thoughts of suicide. Once I explained this to Mary, her obsession with the idea that she might be suicidal quickly diminished. Within a couple of weeks it was gone.

Two factors cause this increased suggestibility. First, anxiety interferes with your ability to reason. This is why the written exercises presented in this book are so important. Writing down your thoughts helps you to analyze critically what you are thinking. Likewise, by putting your rational challenges down on paper you are able to strengthen them in a way that is usually difficult when you are in the middle of an activity.

Increased suggestibility can result also from a childhood where the child is not allowed to disagree with the parents. Previous chapters have detailed how Mary was punished simply for disagreeing with a parent. Robert's parents were so terrifying that he dared not say, do, or think anything that might upset them. As a result, both Mary and Robert began simply to accept whatever their parents said as true, whether it seemed logical or not. In essence, being overly suggestible was reinforced until it became automatic. To use an extreme example, if an abusive parent says, "The sky is green," a child has to make it so and ignore his or her own reason and senses. To do otherwise is to risk the pain of abandonment or punishment.

One way to be less suggestible is to take time to evaluate things that you hear or read. Whenever you become anxious about something, it is a message that you need to use the step-by-step methods you are learning in this book to evaluate your thinking. It is especially helpful to write things down so you can view your worries more objectively. As these skills become more and more automatic, you will find your suggestibility decreasing. Of course, as your overall level of anxiety decreases, you will also find it easier and easier to use your logic. A second way to be less suggestible is learning to trust your judgment. This is discussed in the chapters that follow.

Summary of Key Ideas

1. Desensitization is the process of becoming unresponsive to a stimulus that formerly triggered a conditioned response. Progressive desensitization is the application of this process in a "progressive" manner, starting with situations that trigger the lowest levels of anxiety and slowly working up, or progressing, to those that trigger the highest levels of anxiety.

2. The first step is to make a list of situations that trigger anxiety and rate them as to (1) how much anxiety each one produces and (2) how often you avoid each situation.

3. The second step is to select a specific practice goal and begin practicing regularly. Your first goal needs to be a situation or place that produces a relatively low level of anxiety. It also helps if achieving your first goal has some practical benefit.

4. The third step to complete prior to beginning desensitization is to imagine yourself practicing and make a list of all the fearful physical sensations that might occur along with all of the fearful thoughts that have come up in these types of situations in the past. After the list is completed, develop coping self-statements that address each sensation and fear and write them down on index cards.

5. The fourth step is to begin practicing. Review the cards with your coping self-statements and the nine guidelines for practicing prior to each practice session. If new fearful sensations or thoughts occur, develop additional coping self-statements to deal with them after your practice session.

6. Work through the four-step approach to "what ifs" whenever you have a specific worry.

7. People suffering from severe anxiety tend to be more suggestible. This is usually due to a decrease in the ability to reason caused by the anxiety and by a childhood background where parents allowed little or no disagreement with their views. Take more time to evaluate things using the four-step approach.

Recommended Activities

Make a List of Problem Situations

Follow the examples given in this chapter to create a list of situations that trigger anxiety. Rate each one using the two scales given on page 121. Next, select a specific desensitization goal. Keep in mind that this needs to be something that has a moderate to low rating. It also helps if this goal has some practical benefit.

Develop Specialized Coping Self-Statements

Take a moment to think about being in the situation you have chosen for your desensitization practice. Make a list of all the frightening body sensations you think you might feel. Then make a list of the types of frightening thoughts triggered by this situation.

Once you've compiled your lists, develop a coping self-statement that addresses each item on the lists. When developing coping self-statements for fearful possibilities, be sure you work through the four-step approach to "what ifs."

Begin Desensitizing

After you have completed the first two recommended activities, choose times when you will actually begin your desensitization work. During the first two weeks, be sure to review the practice guidelines and your coping self-statements *before* each practice session. After this, you probably need to review the guidelines only once a week.

Carry your notes and coping cards with you so you can refer to them while you practice. Continue to do this until these skills become an immediate and automatic response to anxiety.

Use Your Journal to Begin Hearing the Message of Anxiety

Continue to use your journal to record times when you are upset. Follow the guidelines given in chapter 7 for identifying and challenging any distorted thinking you are using. You can also use your journal to record how your practice sessions go and work out new coping self-statements whenever a new frightening thought or body sensation occurs.

On days when practicing is more difficult than usual, take a few minutes to record in your journal all of the stresses—physical (sick, hungry, tired), mental, relationship, and spiritual—that are occurring. After several weeks you may see important patterns and identify stresses that increase your symptoms. When this happens, it is usually a message that you need to develop more effective ways of dealing with the problem stress you've identified.

Use the Four-Step Approach to Analyze Your Worries

Take time to write your worries down in your journal and analyze them using the four-step approach outlined in this chapter. Record your conclusions. This will allow you to refer back to your work when these fears resurface. If you're working with a recurring worry, create a coping self-statement and write it on a card that you keep with you.

9

Moving from Basic to Advanced Symptom Control

Achieving Basic Symptom Control

As mentioned previously, the first sessions with Mary, Robert, and Kimberly were devoted to taking a brief history, beginning the development of a simple explanation, and introducing them to as many of the four basic anxiety-reduction skills outlined in chapter 6 as time allowed. Since there is never enough time to do all of this adequately in one session, I gave each of them an audio cassette that explained in more detail the dynamics of anxiety and the four symptom-reducing skills. I also gave them a copy of my book *Anxiety, Phobias, and Panic* and the following homework assignment:

1. Read the written material and listen to the tape that explains in detail the dynamics of anxiety-related problems and the four basic symptom-reducing skills.
2. Rework the simple explanation developed during the session,

putting it in your own words. Change or eliminate anything you don't think applies to you and add anything missing you feel is important.

3. Begin practicing the four basic anxiety-management skills.

The second and third sessions with Mary, Robert, and Kimberly were spent clarifying the dynamics that generate and maintain anxiety, going over the explanation each had developed to make sure it was clear and understood, and helping them apply the basic symptom-reducing skills more effectively.

Mary, Robert, and Kimberly were each responsive to the assigned homework. Each brought in his or her own simple explanation, which you studied in chapter 5, and soon had a good understanding of the dynamics of emotions and anxiety explained in earlier chapters. As each began the work of desensitization he or she moved into the first level of recovery: basic symptom control.

As with most clients, Mary, Robert, and Kimberly were able to reach the level of basic symptom control relatively quickly. Indeed, once a person has a good understanding of how anxiety-related problems develop and are maintained, he or she is able to begin challenging the two main lies that maintain anxiety-related problems: (1) Something dangerous is occurring, and I might go crazy or die, and (2) these symptoms will render me helpless or cause me to do something embarrassing or harmful. Challenging these lies usually helps to bring about some reduction in symptoms, however, it does not eliminate conditioned-response triggers for anxiety or avoidance patterns. It is the work of desensitization that begins to quiet these triggers and to start to move a person from basic symptom control to the next level, advanced symptom control. In addition, a person needs to develop an awareness of at least some of the core beliefs and associations—the message behind the messenger of anxiety—that played a role in the development and maintenance of symptoms.

First Steps to Advanced Symptom Control

Movement to the second level of recovery, advanced symptom control, usually involves a process of taking the skills presented in the previous chapters, developing them over several weeks or months, and adapting them to your individual personality and life situation. As is typical with most clients, the main area of difficulty for Mary, Robert, and Kimberly was applying the information they were given in a concrete way to their daily struggle with anxiety.

Especially difficult for Mary was accepting the idea that anxiety wasn't dangerous. This is a common problem and what helped Mary overcome it was the thought that she had already experienced the worst panic attack she could experience. I had her recall her worst episodes and asked her how she responded to them. She realized that even though she was terrified at those times, she was able to move and think. The attacks did not harm her physically, and even though they seemed very real, the terrible "what ifs" didn't happen. These episodes were just very frightening experiences that left her believing a host of misconceptions about herself and what had happened.

As we identified specific misconceptions, Mary reworked her coping self-statement cards so that they addressed these misconceptions directly. Here is the card she created after our third session and began using along with the one shown in chapter 6.

My initial symptoms left me believing the lie that something was wrong with my body. The symptoms were due to hyperventilation, fear, and being very tired. My doctor confirmed

---

that I am strong and healthy and in great shape. My heart can beat fast with no problem. Any tingling or shortness of breath is just hyperventilation. They are normal responses to fear, and automatic conditioned responses. I now have skills to manage them.

Mary also found it helpful to recall the body sensations she experienced while running marathons and shorter races prior to the onset of her symptoms. This helped her realize that her fear of running was due to her mislabeling normal sensations that felt like the frightening ones. Here is the card she made that addressed this issue:

It is normal to breathe heavily when running. It is also normal for my heart to beat fast. I've experienced these sensations as long as I've run. Because they are similar to sensations I've felt when panicked, I've been mislabeling them as dangerous. They are not dangerous. They are safe and normal. My body is responding to the physical demand of running just as it is supposed to respond.

As a result of the above work, Mary found that within her safe area, the high level of anxiety she had been experiencing reduced to a very low level over the course of about five weeks. Although she still experienced excessive anxiety whenever she was in crowds or ventured more than ten miles from home, or in other situations that were strong triggers, Mary had achieved the first level of recovery, basic symptom control, and was beginning to move to the second level, advanced symptom control.

While Mary could avoid strong triggers and stay in a safe area, Robert had a host of anxiety-provoking triggers at work, plus the primary trigger, eating. As mentioned in the last chapter, this made it important for him to begin working on a program of desensitization while developing the basic symptom-reducing skills. Robert's symptoms did not quiet down as quickly as Mary's, but by the end of the third week, they had lessened enough so that he was able to function again in the area around his office in a fairly normal manner.

One of the greatest stumbling blocks for Robert was his tendency to think that people were watching him closely, noticing his anxiety, and thinking poorly of him. Often, he would imagine that people were talking about him and making jokes about his problem behind his back. Sometimes he would even imagine himself being fired.

It was clear that Robert's childhood fears and memories were fueling his mind reading and catastrophic images. When I asked him for an objective evaluation of his immediate staff, Robert reported that they were actually very nice, supportive people. Robert recalled a time about a year earlier when the child of one of the staff members had a severe illness. During that time, the whole department rallied around that staff member and were very thoughtful. Robert also recalled how the conversations held behind this person's back were sympathetic ones. As a result of this, he developed the following coping self-statement card:

While I may be anxious, there is nothing wrong with me physically or mentally. My anxiety is just a holdover from all of the lies I've been telling myself and the many conditioned-response triggers I've developed.

I can talk and do my job even when I'm anxious. I've been doing this for quite some time now. No one pays that much attention to my anxiety. Most probably don't even notice or they think that that's just the way I am. They're too busy with work and their own problems to pay much attention to my symptoms.

Even if someone notices, they all know the pressure I've been under to complete this project. They usually just attribute symptoms in others as due to stress. They will do the same with me.

My secretary is very supportive and sympathetic. She is not thinking badly of me.

Just take things slowly. Do as much and go as far as you can. People are too wrapped up in their own business to pay much attention to you.

Here is an additional card Robert made that addressed the time tunnel aspect of his excessive concern with how others thought:

When I get anxious I'm just replaying an old tape from childhood—I'm time tunneling.

Keep in mind that the feelings you have about people thinking poorly of you are just holdovers from childhood. My parents belittled me and thought poorly of me. These people are not my parents. They are co-workers and subordinates. I'm no longer a child. I'm a supervisor and an adult.

Many of these people respond to me as an authority figure. I have power and choices I didn't have as a child.

Confronting Death and Uncertainty

Kimberly used the same basic tools and cognitive-behavioral approach as Mary and Robert. However, because her symptoms were due to posttraumatic stress disorder, the issues she needed to address were different. It turned out that Kimberly had three key issues that she had to work through. The first was the fact that her mortality and her inability to control many circumstances in her life had become more of an immediate reality.

One of the ways we cope with danger is simply to ignore it. Once you have a life-threatening experience, thought, you can no longer ignore the potential for danger, at least in similar situations. This is one of the chief reasons we become more cautious as we get older. Young people simply haven't had as many experiences where they felt they were in danger. It's easy for them simply to ignore the dangers of driving fast or doing other potentially harmful activities. As you mature, you experience harm firsthand, or see friends and loved ones experience it in various situations. This gives a reality to danger and to our inability to control many events that was not present before.

Over time, we also become increasingly aware of the fact that we are mortal and someday will die. Young people tend to act and think as if they will live forever. As you age, you begin to notice your body losing the resiliency of youth. More aches and pains develop. You also begin to experience the death of people you know. This last event frequently is a shock. In the past, death due to childhood diseases, injuries, infections, and genetic defects was more common. In our modern world, many people don't experience the death of a friend or loved one until they are adults. Indeed, the death of a close friend or loved one is one of the factors that triggers the onset of severe anxiety in many of my clients.

In Kimberly's case, she had a life-threatening experience. This ordeal was the result of another person's actions; it was unpredictable, and it definitely *was* dangerous. Prior to this, she thought she could handle anything, and that nothing could happen to her. The assault shattered that belief. The fact that several people had been injured in her district that year became much more real to her. Kimberly came to therapy thinking that once she "got over" her problem, she would be able to return to her old way of thinking and dealing with life. This was an unrealistic expectation.

Because Kimberly had to rethink her beliefs about death and her physical limitations, this became a recurring topic during our sessions. Initially, Kimberly was faced with the choice of either deciding to transfer to a position that was less dangerous or to adjust to the idea that she would have to be more aware and cautious in the future. As we focused on this reality, Kimberly began to realize how much she was beating herself up for being "weak." She did this because of the two childhood beliefs: "Mistakes are not acceptable" and "I must be strong and never show weakness."

Challenging these erroneous core beliefs became the second major area of work for Kimberly. She found the idea that she was "a *normal person* who was in an *abnormal situation*" especially helpful. This, along with the knowledge of how the mind reacts to trauma presented in chapter 3, helped her understand that her mind needed time to process the assault. The fact that anyone traumatized severely enough would have similar symptoms helped her begin to think of herself as normal. She especially liked the idea that flashbacks were simply "snapshots" that the mind was looking at one at a time in order to "process" the event.

Also important to Kimberly's therapy was her understanding of the conditioned-response nature of her reaction. She had spent her life thinking that she could "will" herself to do anything and respond however she wanted to respond. This was the first time that she fully realized that there were some situations where will-power simply didn't work. By becoming alarmed when she could not "will" away the conditioned-response anxiety triggered by people or situations similar to those present during the assault, she was actually *increasing* her symptoms. Kimberly loved the relaxation-response tape I gave her and was amazed at how well she responded to it. This response not only gave her needed relief from her symptoms but also helped her see how strong and automatic conditioned responses can be.

Here is the card that Kimberly developed that incorporated these three ideas:

I used to think I was indestructible and that nothing serious would ever happen to me. The assault has opened my eyes to the fact that this is not true. This does not make me a wimp or somehow less of a person. It only means I'm more experienced in life and will assess dangers more realistically.

Any person who is traumatized like I was will experience posttraumatic stress symptoms.

I'm a *normal person* who has experienced an *abnormal situation*. Because of this, I'm having normal reactions to something that was too much for me to handle all at once.

The anxiety and flashbacks I sometimes experience are not a sign of being weak willed. Conditioned responses can occur no matter how strong willed you are. Quit beating yourself up and just use your skills. You have already seen them work.

During the first month, Kimberly continued to experience regular flashbacks and excessive anxiety whenever she encountered something that reminded her of the assault. However, her symptoms reduced greatly during normal activities, and she began to regain confidence in herself.

Shame

Another factor that keeps people stuck at the first level of recovery and focused on symptoms is shame. Shame is usually defined as a painful emotion caused by a strong sense of guilt, embarrassment, unworthiness, or disgrace. Within the model of emotions presented in chapter 4, shame is due to a sense of loss, and, therefore, a type of sadness. The loss that triggers shame is the perceived loss of one's reputation or the tainting of one's identity. In essence, shame comes from the perception that one has been "stained" in some way. This can be due to an event such as a rape or childhood molestation or to a core belief that causes the perception that one is inferior to others in a significant way. Often, as with Mary, Robert, and Kimberly, shame is triggered by both types of loss. For example, the assault that triggered Kimberly's posttraumatic stress disorder was not only a stain on her reputation but also evidence that she didn't measure up to the unrealistic expectation that she "should" be able to handle anything. In Mary's and Robert's cases, their panic disorder both confirmed the core belief from childhood that they were inadequate and did not measure up to others and served as a lasting "mark" of that inadequacy that everyone could see.

One of the keys to long-term recovery is realizing that everyone has weaknesses and struggles. They are just a part of the human condition and experience. If you have a sensitive body or have experienced something extraordinary, it is normal to experience the symptoms of anxiety. This "normalizing" of oneself is also the key to overcoming the sense of shame that goes along with not only anxiety-related problems but a host of problems that people face. As Mary, Robert, and Kimberly came slowly to redefine what it meant to be human and what was normal, they found their sense of shame gradually lifted. As you will read in the chapters that follow, one of the main tasks for them in achieving this was to challenge core beliefs from childhood that either demanded impossibly high standards or that identified Mary, Robert, and Kimberly as inadequate in some way.

Summary of Key Ideas

1. The basic skills presented in chapters 5 through 8 need to be adapted to your individual personality and life situation.
2. While basic symptom control is achieved fairly quickly, it usually takes several weeks or months to move to advanced symptom control. So, be patient.
3. A person usually needs to overcome several stumbling blocks in order to achieve advanced symptom control. These vary widely from person to person. This chapter presented the following five:
   - It takes time to convince yourself that anxiety isn't dangerous.
   - The childhood message "I don't measure up" can cause the belief that others think poorly of you.
   - It's difficult to come to grips with our mortality and our inability to control many of life's circumstances.
   - It is difficult to accept the conditioned-response aspect of severe anxiety and learn that your goal is to manage it rather than eliminate it. Managing it is the key to desensitization, which leads to symptom reduction.
   - It takes time to replace deep-seated lies with the truth.

4. Shame is a painful emotion caused by a strong sense of guilt, embarrassment, unworthiness, or disgrace that is due to a sense of loss, and, therefore, a type of sadness.

5. The key to overcoming shame is to challenge core beliefs from childhood that either demanded impossibly high standards or that identify you as inadequate in some way. This is a part of learning to see yourself as normal.

Recommended Activities

Identify Your Key Stumbling Blocks and Develop Coping Self-Statements That Address Them

In the previous chapters you have identified core beliefs and associations that played a role in the development and maintenance of your symptoms. Use the models presented in this chapter to develop a card that addresses each issue you've identified. Review this card daily for at least two weeks. If you have not yet identified core beliefs and associations that play a role in your symptoms, review chapter 4 and do the recommended activities it suggests.

Repetition, Repetition, Repetition

As you read through these case examples, it is important to keep in mind that the work described in this chapter covered a period of many weeks. Mary's acceptance that anxiety was not dangerous, for example, did not come about as the result of one session. As she practiced desensitization, and we together worked on other issues, we would periodically go over the information presented at the beginning of this chapter. Mary would leave the session confident that anxiety was not dangerous. However, after a short time, sometimes only a few hours, the old fears would wash over her and drown out this truth. As we went over the ideas in subsequent sessions, and she began to use the coping self-statements that addressed this issue directly, she slowly became convinced that it was true.

When you have believed a lie and repeated it to yourself over and over, it takes time to convince yourself of the truth. In order for the truth to become a conviction that is stronger than the lies you've been telling yourself, you may need to reread several times the sections of this book that address the lies that drive your anxiety.

If you had a difficult childhood, many of the defenses you developed to cope with childhood problems may be interfering with your ability to look at yourself objectively. When this is the case, it takes much repetition and persistence to penetrate these defenses.

Use Your Journal to Challenge Problem Core Beliefs and Associations

It is now time to begin putting together the different pieces of the previous chapters. If you have not yet begun to write in a journal for at least fifteen minutes every other day, review the suggestions given in the "Recommended Activities" section of chapters 4, 5, and 8.

As you record your self-talk when you are upset, identify the underlying beliefs or associations supporting the distorted thinking that is present then. These will usually be the core beliefs and associations you identified while doing the recommended activities in chapter 4. If you have not done them, go back and do them now.

In essence, you are now working at two different levels. The first is simply to develop logical challenges for the various forms of distorted thinking you use, as was described in chapter 7. The second is to identify the underlying beliefs and associations upon which the surface self-talk is based, as described in this chapter. While this second task is more difficult, once you become skilled at it, you will find it a powerful tool.

If you're finding it very difficult to identify and challenge core beliefs and associations, you may need someone to help you. This person could be a friend, a relative, a fellow sufferer whom you trust, or a professional therapist. Remember that it is usually easier to see others objectively than it is to see yourself.

Continue Desensitization

If you have avoidance patterns or situations that provoke severe anxiety, continue practicing systematic desensitization as discussed in the last chapter. Keep in mind that you need to repeat a given practice activity many times before you move on to a new goal. Also, keep in mind the conditioned-response nature of much of your anxiety. Understanding why your anxiety is triggered will not stop a given situation from activating it. Only time and continued, systematic practice will do that.

10

Establishing Healthy Boundaries

One of the drawbacks in writing a book like this one is the need to summarize in a few pages work that often takes weeks or months to accomplish. This can give the impression that a client comes to a session, gains an important insight, learns a new skill, goes out and applies it, then lives happily ever after. If only it were so easy! Achieving long-term recovery actually takes many months, and even years, depending upon how many issues are intertwined with the anxiety symptoms and whether or not you are using an effective approach.

Complex learning is always accomplished through a series of steps over time. Consider how long it takes to learn to read and write. Even when an adult is learning this skill, it usually takes several months for him or her to be able to read comfortably at a sixth-grade level. Compared to changing complex habit patterns that have been ingrained for many years, learning to read is easy!

What Are Boundaries in Human Relationships?

When applied to human relationships, a boundary refers to the limits we place on relationships. As we grow and develop, we learn to set limits on how much of ourselves we disclose to others, to what extent we allow others to influence us, what we will do to others, and what we will allow others to do to us. These limits can be thought of as our personal boundaries.

The person with *weak boundaries* is like a piece of property with little or no fencing. Anyone can walk in and out with little resistance, taking or leaving whatever they want. The person with *rigid boundaries* is like a piece of property with high, thick walls and no gates. Nothing gets in, and nothing gets out. In contrast, a person with *healthy boundaries* is like a piece of property with a strong wall and a gate that can be easily opened or closed by the owner depending upon who is approaching and what the approaching person wants. The gate is opened to receive people who have proven themselves trustworthy and whose requests seem reasonable. Similarly it is closed when people approaching are hurtful or are making inappropriate requests.

In order to have healthy boundaries you need to be able to:

- recognize when your boundaries are being ignored by others;
- identify what you can do to establish healthy boundaries in a given situation; and
- use assertive skills to enforce your boundaries.

Missing Anxiety's Message

The concept of boundaries takes us back to one of the central themes of this book: Anxiety is a messenger. Unfortunately, when they have been ignored for years, messages about boundary violations are difficult to recognize. Mary presents a good example of this.

After several months of therapy, Mary's symptoms had reduced considerably and she was able to do more and more of the things that had been difficult for her when she first came to me. She was moving from the level of basic symptom control to a high level of advanced symptom control. Since much of the work at this stage is in the area of systematic desensitization and applying the skills presented in the previous chapters to everyday situations, we were now meeting only every three weeks. During one session Mary came in and reported that after doing well for several weeks, her symptoms had begun to increase and she was finding it difficult to practice. I asked her if anything unusual had happened, and she reported that everything in her life was just as it had been before.

Things often seem to be going well for a client when, all of a sudden, symptoms seem to escalate for no apparent reason. Closer examination usually reveals a logical explanation. In order to understand the increase in Mary's symptoms, I asked her to give me a detailed account of daily events starting just before her symptoms began to increase. In describing the previous week, she mentioned in passing, "My mother's birthday is in two weeks, and my brother called to arrange a family get-together."

Because Mary had described so much pain associated with her family, this simple statement became a giant red flag. Indeed, as we began to discuss this upcoming get-together, Mary realized that she was very anxious about it. It had been some time since she had seen her family all together. Furthermore, she began to recall how abusively she was treated at family gatherings. As the cause of the increase in Mary's anxiety became clear, she became puzzled as to why she had missed it.

As a child, Mary viewed her parents' inappropriate behavior as normal. Since there was nothing she could do to stop her family's abusive treatment, she learned to become numb to it. Ignoring the rejection and emotional pain associated with her mother also allowed Mary to obtain the small amount of positive attention that her mother was able to give her. Ignoring was also the way in which both Mary's father and mother dealt with difficult emotional issues. Thus, the rule "Don't look, don't feel, run away" can be seen as something that Mary learned not only due to necessity, but by example.

Mary's perception of her family's abusive behavior as normal, and her ability to bury the hurt associated with her family, had become so automatic that she had immediately pushed out of consciousness the fact that the upcoming time with her mother would be painful. However, the pain she connected with her mother and the deep-seated belief that Mary would be helpless to protect herself from her family were realities that, on an unconscious level, could not be ignored. The result was an increase in her anxiety symptoms as her fight-or-flight response was triggered.

Because Mary had learned to become numb to her family's abusive behavior and had carried this defense mechanism into adulthood, she was unable to hear the message being conveyed by her anxiety: she needed to decide what she was going to do about the upcoming family event. Did she want to participate in an event that would be painful? If she decided to attend, she needed to develop a plan for coping with the hurtful behavior of her family—a plan for enforcing her personal boundaries.

If you have important issues from childhood that you learned to ignore or label as normal, you probably have times when your symptoms seem to increase for no apparent reason. When this occurs, take a moment to see if there are any significant family-related events or commemorative dates, such as birthdays or anniversaries, coming up. If so, it may be that the upcoming event or date has triggered anxiety related to family issues.

Another common experience is "holiday anxiety." Many people who come from dysfunctional families find that their symptoms increase around Thanksgiving, decrease a little, then increase again as Christmas approaches. Their symptoms then remain at a high level until after New Year's Day. The cause for this is simple. The increased tension of the holiday season often makes parents with limited coping skills become more abusive during the holidays. A critical parent, for example, becomes more critical, while a physically abusive parent becomes more out of control.

When holiday decorations and music are associated with pain during a person's childhood, they tend to trigger the reexperiencing of childhood anxieties when that person is an adult. This phenomenon is so common I often tell clients who are experiencing holiday anxiety, "You'll probably feel much better around January 15th." As they begin to feel better after the holidays, many are amazed at my "predictive" ability. However, a quick review of the causes of holiday anxiety makes this prediction less remarkable. What is amazing is how blind we can be to key issues.

What Should I Do?

Mary's family had a long history of ignoring her boundaries. This was especially true of her mother, who was very critical, asked inappropriate personal questions, and frequently made inappropriate requests. As we discussed this, Mary decided that the most hurtful behaviors during the gathering would likely be the result of her mother's drinking. Her mother's usual pattern was to begin drinking just before dinner, continue drinking after dinner, and become increasingly verbally abusive as the evening wore on. This, in turn, usually caused all of the other members of the family to become very hurtful toward one another, and especially toward Mary.

At this point Mary decided that she really *did* want to see her family. Even though she is an intelligent woman with good judgment, she wasn't sure how she could protect herself from their painful behavior. The reason for her difficulty was the childhood message "I'm not as intelligent or capable as others and can't do anything correctly," which caused her to doubt her ability to figure things out and come up with good solutions. Since people who find it difficult to think clearly about their own problems often have the ability to see the problems of others objectively, I asked Mary, "What would you tell a friend who was having this problem?"

Mary decided that her "friend" needed to get an inexpensive motel room so she could leave right after dinner if her mother started to become abusive. I then said, "That sounds like it might also work for you." At first, Mary found it difficult to see how a solution that would be appropriate for a friend would be appropriate for her. After a little thought and discussion, she began to see how this idea was exactly what she needed to do.

Next, we discussed ways in which Mary could protect herself while she was around her family. Since she was not yet feeling strong enough to confront her mother directly, she developed several socially acceptable excuses for leaving when things became too uncomfortable. In addition, Mary and I developed several strategies for changing the subject in case a topic came up that promoted criticism from her parents or brothers.

In the weeks that followed, whenever Mary described a situation in which she was confused as to what an appropriate boundary should be, as a starting point I asked her what she would tell a friend with this problem. After doing this for several weeks, Mary found that she began to trust her judgment more and more.

If you doubt your ability to respond to a difficult interpersonal situation, use this same approach and pretend you are talking to a friend who has asked for your advice. Try to come up with the best possible solution. Like Mary, you will probably come up with a pretty good solution. If you find it difficult to use this approach, or to accept that your solution is a good one, consult with someone who has proven to be reliable and clear thinking. See what he or she thinks of the solution you've developed. While he or she might have useful additions, you'll probably find that you have a stronger ability to develop appropriate answers yourself than you had previously believed. You just simply didn't trust your ability.

As Mary worked out a specific plan for all the anxiety-producing situations connected with the family event she could think of, her symptoms lessened substantially. Nevertheless, her anxiety remained at a higher level than it had been prior to her learning about the event. This is normal; the event was a major challenge for Mary. After the get-together, it took two weeks for her anxiety to return to its previous level, and for her to feel that she was again making substantial progress. This is also normal. The emotional stress of this event was similar to being sick with a bad cold or the flu. Mary's body was drained, and it took time for it to regain its physical and emotional strength.

One other activity Mary found helpful was to act as an observer during some of the time she spent with her family. When she simply observed her family's interaction in as objective a manner as she could, she was amazed at what she saw. The insights she gained proved very useful in the weeks to come when she challenged old beliefs about herself and her place in the world.

If you are going to be around your family, you might also find it useful to spend some time observing their behavior and interactions. Pretend that you are a research scientist studying how your family members treat one another. You might also want to try to identify the unspoken rules that guide their interactions. You'll probably be surprised at what you find.

Honoring Your Rights

The final step in developing appropriate boundaries is learning how to be assertive. Usually, the two biggest roadblocks are a poor self-image and thoughts about yourself and others that cause you to believe that you have no right to protect or assert yourself. The result is that even a person who knows how to be assertive will find it difficult to use those skills in at least some situations. *Situational nonassertiveness* like this usually involves situations with parents, spouses, authority figures, siblings, or close friends. It was this lack of belief in her rights that made it difficult for Mary to see that the solutions that were appropriate for her "friend" were also appropriate for her.

Even a cursory glance at Mary's background, as given in chapter 2, makes clear how she developed her sense of not having any rights. In the weeks after our initial session, Mary recalled many ways in which she was treated with disrespect while growing up. For example, when her brothers teased her or were mean, her mother would ignore the situation or tell her, "Don't make such a big deal out of things." Mary even remembered several incidents where she tried to express an opinion that differed from her mother's and was told, "You've got no right to think like that."

One of the activities Mary found helpful was to develop a list of "rights" that were difficult for her to affirm. She wrote these on a card and read them to herself two or three times a day for a month. By the end of the month, she found that it was much easier both to identify boundary violations and to take action to set appropriate limits. Here is the card she developed:

I have the right to be treated with dignity and respect.

I have the right to decide what is best for me.

I have the right to have and express my own feelings and opinions.

I have the right to ask for what I want and need.

I have the right to say "no" without feeling guilty.

I have the right to be listened to and taken seriously.

I have the right to do what is necessary to protect my physical and mental health, even though this sometimes causes discomfort to others.

The Excessive Need for Approval

Another factor that causes a person to have weak boundaries and be nonassertive is an excessive need for approval. It is normal and healthy to want others to like and approve of you. You can't have a healthy relationship unless there is some desire to please the other person. At the same time, this need can become so exaggerated that it destroys relationships and causes you to ignore other important needs. An excessive need for approval usually comes from growing up in a home where the needs of a child to feel loved and important were inadequately met.

When you have an excessive need for approval, you tend to

avoid doing anything that will cause disapproval. In fact, the excessive need for approval, often referred to as a fear of rejection or fear of abandonment, plays a major role in the development of weak boundaries and nonassertive behavior. Whenever you assert yourself or tell someone "no," there is the possibility that others might reject you or disapprove of you. For someone with an excessive need for approval this can be too great a risk to take.

Two common traits frequently connected with an excessive need for approval are *indecision* and *difficulty accepting criticism*. Indecision is due to the fear that a wrong decision might bring disapproval; difficulty accepting criticism results because criticism tends to be seen as rejection, even when it is given in a constructive manner.

Two additional problems associated with an excessive need for approval are *excessive dependency* and *jealousy*. A person with these traits is often overly demanding of friends' or a mate's time and attention. When they see someone important to them spending time with someone else, they may become jealous because this person is "stealing" the attention they are so dependent upon.

Mary and Robert both had an excessive need for approval. While Mary was not troubled with jealousy, she did have a big problem with weak boundaries and being nonassertive. Robert, on the other hand, had developed fairly rigid boundaries as a means of protecting himself as a child. At the same time, he described many incidents where he was very jealous and demanding in his relationships. While Robert was able to be fairly assertive in his role as a supervisor, he was often not so with his wife and close friends. More is said about assertiveness in the next chapter.

Summary Sheets

Because you are working to change deeply ingrained beliefs and habit patterns, you will tend to forget important insights and new skills. This is normal. New knowledge and skills often need to be relearned several times before they are fully internalized. *Summary sheets* are an excellent method you can use to make this process easier. A summary sheet is a page that addresses one specific core belief, association, or behavior that you have identified as an underlying recurring problem.

To create a summary sheet, begin by listing the core belief, association, or behavior at the top of the page. Then create the following sections:

- Why this is an issue
- Situations where this causes problems
- Things I can tell myself
- Things I can do

Here is the summary sheet that Robert created to deal with the issue of approval:

THE EXCESSIVE NEED FOR APPROVAL

Why This Is an Issue
My parents were so broken that they were unable to give me the love I needed as a child. They were often cold and rejecting. While I developed rigid walls to protect myself, I still desperately wanted their love.

Situations Where This Causes Problems
1. When my wife goes to a work function or off with her friends, I tend to feel abandoned and rejected by her. In the past I became angry and would nitpick and criticize her before and after events like these.
2. When I see my wife or one of my good friends talking with

---

someone in a social situation, I tend to barge in and dominate the conversation.

3. I often have difficulty telling my wife what I want. When we have a disagreement I tend to crawl back into my shell and stop talking.
4. I tend to react to criticism badly, whether it is a job review or simple advice from a friend. I'll either withdraw or lash out.

Things I Can Tell Myself
Rejection and disapproval are a part of life. While I don't like them and would prefer everyone to like me, I don't have to fear them. Most of the disapproval and rejection I experience has little to do with me. The other person is either sick, hungry, tired, or angry at something or someone other than me. I also know that others often time tunnel as I do and withdraw because they are mixing me and the present with their past. The bottom line is that there will always be some who won't like me no matter what I do, just as there are people I don't like. As for my friends, wife, and child, rejection is a *temporary* part of any healthy relationship. Sometimes the rejection I feel is really me rejecting myself or feeling down on myself.

Things I Can Do
1. The most important thing for me to do is *stop and think* when I begin to feel jealous or hurt. I will take a moment to ask the two time tunnel questions, "What's happening?" and "What is real?"
2. When I feel jealous in a social situation, and notice myself taking over, I will be quiet and remember the arguments above. I will practice listening.
3. When I have an argument or disagreement with my wife, I will take a time-out and use the assertive skills I'm learning

to approach the disagreement in a problem-solving manner.

4. When I receive criticism, I will not say anything until I have time to think about it. As I think about it I will ask the following questions:

   a. Is this something that is important enough that I want to even consider it?

   b. Is this person a reliable source for this issue?

   c. Was this criticism offered in a constructive or hurtful manner?

   d. Look at the criticism objectively. Is it valid?

Summary of Key Ideas

1. People from dysfunctional families often have either weak or rigid boundaries.
2. Establishing healthy boundaries requires that you:

   - learn to recognize when your boundaries are being violated;
   - identify what you can do in a given situation to establish an appropriate boundary; and
   - develop assertive skills to enforce appropriate boundaries.

3. It's often difficult to hear the "message" anxiety sends because it deals with an issue that you've trained yourself to ignore.
4. People from dysfunctional families often find that holidays and anniversaries trigger the reexperiencing of childhood anxieties.
5. It's important to develop concrete plans for protecting yourself when you are going to be around family members who act inappropriately.
6. One of the main roadblocks to being assertive is a message

from childhood that reinforces the belief that you have few or no rights in relationships.

7. The excessive need for approval is a common problem for people with severe anxiety.

8. Create summary sheets for core beliefs and associations that generate dysfunctional thoughts and behaviors.

Recommended Activities

Continue to Practice Desensitization

If you have avoidance patterns, it is *essential* that you practice systematic desensitization. This is a proven method that works!

Challenge Irrational Beliefs about Assertiveness

This chapter pointed out that one of the main roadblocks to being assertive is usually the presence of irrational beliefs about assertiveness. Several common ones are listed below. Check any that describe how you think or act.

- It is wrong and selfish to refuse the requests of others.
- I don't need to ask for what I want since others should know without my asking.
- If I disagree with others, they will become angry or upset with me.
- If someone becomes angry or upset, I may not be able to handle the situation.

- If others become angry or upset, they might reject or abandon me.
- If I ask questions or say what I think, I might say something that makes me look stupid or ignorant.
- I prefer others to be open and straightforward with me. However, I will hurt them if I'm straightforward and open with them.
- If I say or do something that hurts others, I am responsible for their feelings regardless of my intentions and how I acted. (Common variation: I should be able to act in a way that will not hurt others.)

Beliefs such as the above usually develop during childhood. Take the time to think about each of the following questions. Record your answers in your journal.

- How did each member of your family deal with conflict?
- How did the adults who raised you train you to deal with conflict?
- What was the main message you got about conflict?
- Did your brothers and sisters receive the same training and the same messages you did? If not, how were they different?
- How did you get what you wanted indirectly (for example, by hinting, whining, sulking, or having someone else ask for you)?
- Did you learn how to get what you wanted in other ways?
- Which of these methods do you use today to get what you want?
- What types of messages or statements do you repeat to yourself when you are in conflict with others?

As you identify your irrational beliefs about being assertive, develop rational responses you can use to challenge them.

Learn Your "Rights"

Review the list of rights Mary used on page 161. If any of them describes an area where you have difficulty, write it on a card and read it two or three times a day for a month.

Learn to Recognize When Your Boundaries Are Being Violated

People struggling with anxiety often find that remembering that anxiety is a messenger is the key to recognizing the times when boundaries are being violated. While not all anxiety is due to boundary violations, anxiety is usually the first indication that a boundary violation is happening. Whenever anxiety occurs for what seems like no apparent reason, ask yourself, "Has someone violated my boundaries or am I approaching a situation where my boundaries might be violated?"

Begin Creating "Summary Sheets" for Recurring Key Issues

By now, you have probably identified one or more core beliefs or associations that generate recurring problems. Create a summary sheet for each one using the format described in this chapter. Review your summary sheet once a day for at least two weeks. As you identify new situations where this issue causes problems, add them to your sheet. Also, add any new thoughts or actions you discover that help you respond in new and healthier ways. After you've spent two weeks reviewing your sheet daily, put it in a safe place so you can review it in the future when this issue again causes problems.

Remember the "New Car Principle"

An amazing thing I've noticed every time I've bought a new car is how many other cars of the same make and model I begin to see. The reason is simple. The purchase of the new car "fixed" the car's image in my mind so that other cars like it seemed to stand out.

This principle is important to keep in mind when you do the various recommended activities. Reviewing a summary sheet or a "rights" card daily for two or more weeks "fixes" these ideas in your mind. Then, just as the purchase of a new car helps you see similar cars everywhere you look, the daily review helps you see when you are using old behaviors and thinking patterns. Becoming aware of these old patterns then allows you to substitute the new ones you wish to establish. In time, these new patterns become as automatic as the old ones.

11

Detours along the Path to Recovery

The path from advanced symptom control to long-term recovery often has several detours. This can be discouraging, as it is both normal and healthy to want the process of recovery to move along more quickly than it does. No one wants to struggle with the issues described in this book. Indeed, if it were simply a matter of desensitizing oneself to conditioned responses as discussed in chapter 8, recovery would be a fairly simple and straightforward process. Unfortunately, these conditioned responses usually become intertwined with core beliefs and associations from childhood, factors that developed over many years and that are often slow to change. The good news is that the healing process initiated by severe anxiety can nurture growth and development that allows for a much richer and more enjoyable life than was possible prior to the development of one's symptoms.

Practice, Practice, Practice

While Robert was working at desensitizing himself to those areas at work that had become anxiety provoking, we also set up a desensitization schedule that included the gradual reintroduction of solid foods. Beginning with soft foods such as bananas, Robert worked systematically up to more troublesome foods such as meats and vegetables. Once he understood the desensitization process, he made rapid progress. After six weeks, he was eating a fairly wide range of foods and was again able to function effectively at work. He was still unable to go into restaurants or the company cafeteria, and he still had high levels of anxiety during meetings and when traveling out of town, but there was marked improvement. He clearly had achieved the first level of recovery, basic symptom control, and was moving toward the second level, advanced symptom control.

Robert's next goal was to eat in restaurants. To accomplish this, we set up a desensitization program where he would begin visiting yogurt shops, then progress on to donut shops, pancake houses, fast-food restaurants, and, finally, regular restaurants. Six weeks later, Robert was going to fast-food restaurants for breakfast with no difficulty, and was able to eat most foods at home with the exception of salsa and chips, something he had formerly enjoyed. It took another three months before Robert felt comfortable eating out, but he practiced regularly and closely followed the guidelines given in chapter 8.

What accounted for Robert's steady progress? First, he practiced regularly. One of the main reasons clients remain stuck in avoidance patterns is lack of practice. It cannot be emphasized too much: You need to practice regularly. It is the *only* way you will desensitize and *know* that you can do something.

Second, Robert used his journal to develop customized coping self-statements whenever new fears or troubling thoughts developed. The basic coping self-statements presented in chapter 6, such as "Anxiety is not dangerous" or "I can be anxious and still function," are important first steps. However, to achieve long-term recovery you need to go beyond them and address the other underlying core beliefs and associations that generate distorted thinking and problem behaviors.

In chapter 9 you saw that one of Robert's problem behaviors was excessive worry about what others were thinking of him. The description of Robert's childhood background presented in chapter 2 revealed that he was constantly teased at school and put down at home, resulting in a poor self-image. Chapter 4 detailed three of Robert's negative core beliefs: "Conflict is dangerous," "Something is wrong with me. I'm inferior to others," and "People always let you down." Each of these played a role in Robert's symptoms and needed to be addressed within his rational self-talk. Reread Robert's coping self-statements given in chapter 9 and his summary sheet at the end of chapter 10. Note how Robert is already beginning to challenge these basic assumptions as part of his rational response.

In addition, Mary, Robert, and Kimberly all applied the "new car principle" described in the "Recommended Activities" section of chapter 10 and faithfully read their summary sheets and coping cards until they could easily recall them. Each time they identified a new problem belief or association, they created a new card or summary sheet and reviewed it until these healthier patterns were automatic. For example, Robert discovered that he often was pessimistic about future events, so he created the following summary sheet:

THE LIE THAT THINGS WILL ALWAYS BE THE SAME

Why This Is an Issue
My childhood was a series of painful events. Both of my parents were also very negative and pessimistic. Because of this I developed the belief that there was no reason to hope that my life would get better; things would always turn out poorly.

Situations Where This Causes Problems
I often find it difficult to plan for the future. When others are discussing their plans, I tend to be critical and point out all the things that can go wrong. My expectation that events will go poorly causes me to focus on small, negative things that occur and prevents me from enjoying life.

Things I Can Tell Myself
My past has no control over my future. Although my memories and past conditioned-response associations do cause old feelings to surface, they are only emotions from events that no longer exist. The power to change things is now, in the present. Because I cannot predict the future, I do not really know what each day has in store for me. In the past I believed that the painful things I'd experienced would "always" repeat themselves. But, this is the lie. Things are always changing. If I change my beliefs and behavior, I will see a change in how I feel and respond. I will also see a change in other people and events.

Things I Can Do
1. Choose to identify and focus on what is going well.
2. When I notice small things that are not the way I like them, I can identify them as simply small inconveniences and refocus on something positive.
3. Keep quiet when people discuss their plans about future

events except to say things such as "That sounds exciting" or "That sounds like fun."

4. Stay away from people who are negative and spend more time with positive people.
5. Read uplifting and positive material.

During the early part of her therapy, Mary often found it difficult to practice. She thought of this in terms of being afraid to go outside of her "comfort zone" and created this summary sheet.

FEAR OF GOING OUTSIDE MY "COMFORT ZONE"

Why This Is an Issue
As a child, the criticism and put-downs by my parents and brothers caused me to believe the lie that "I'm not as intelligent or capable as others." My gentle nature, the constant teasing of my brothers, and my mother's constant warnings also caused me to believe the lie that "The world is too dangerous for me. I'm not safe."

Situations Where This Causes Problems
These lies have caused me to try to create a small, safe world and to avoid taking risks. The biggest problem this is causing me at present is my reluctance to do the work needed to desensitize.

Things I Can Tell Myself
While there are many dangers in the world, I'm an intelligent and capable adult. I'm *not* a helpless little girl. I know how to take reasonable precautions and get help when I need it. I do not need to hide in my safe little world any longer. It's time to

move out of my comfort zone and take my place in the world as an adult.

Things I Can Do
1. Choose to practice regularly.
2. Review this summary sheet regularly.
3. Remind myself of the rewards that practicing brings: freedom, a more positive self-image, more opportunities in work and friendships, and more joy.

In a similar manner, you need to identify the key issues that create problems in your life and address them in a concrete manner over a period of time.

Relearning Is Easier Than Starting from Scratch

As with Mary and Robert, Kimberly experienced her own detours on the road to recovery. After three months, her symptoms were greatly reduced. She had remained home from work due to her injuries and had gone through several cycles of intense anxiety and anger, and moderate depression, which is normal for an active, dynamic individual like Kimberly who has experienced major physical and psychological trauma.

Because Kimberly was making good progress, we met less frequently. One day, after several weeks of good progress, she was talking with a fellow employee on the telephone and learned that a student had hit another employee with a coffee cup. She came to me a few days later and reported that her symptoms had intensified considerably and she was again having nightmares about

OVERCOMING ANXIETY

being assaulted. Kimberly understood how the report had restimulated the memories of her own assault. Nonetheless, she did not realize that they also were making her concerns about the possibility of being reinjured at work even more real.

Chapter 9 discussed Kimberly's difficulty in dealing with her mortality and her inability to control many circumstances in her life. After a couple of months, her symptoms had decreased enough so that she was no longer regularly using the rational self-talk described in that chapter. She had been keeping busy with family activities and had put the question of whether she would return to work or seek a different position at the back of her mind. The incident brought this important question to the forefront again. In essence, the increased symptoms she was experiencing had two messages: First, she needed to return to the basic skills and desensitize herself to the flare-up of anxiety that was triggered by this new violent incident. Second, she needed to decide what she was going to do about work.

When real-life experiences trigger old anxiety patterns, the first thing I have clients do is pull out the simple explanation and basic coping self-statements they created during the early phase of their treatment. Next, I have them review their summary sheets. Since it's easy to forget the skills and insights you've learned, I encourage you to do the recommended activities at the end of each chapter in your journal so you can refer back to them in the future. Although the goal of this work is to get to the point where the skills become automatic, it's easy to slip into old negative patterns when symptoms recur. Because of this, you need to return to the basics, and apply your skills in a systematic and conscious manner. It usually takes several cycles of forgetting what you've learned and going back through the basics before these skills and insights are internalized enough to become automatic. Fortunately, relearning is usually easier than learning something for the first time and having a written record of what you've done makes it even easier.

Kimberly reviewed the basic skills, and began using them in a systematic manner. She began feeling better in about a week, but the question of what to do about returning to work continued to plague her. One of the chief causes of her difficulty in resolving this issue was the message from childhood "I must be strong and never show weakness." During one of our sessions, Kimberly realized that she was equating changing her job with being weak, just as she had viewed her symptoms as a sign of being weak willed. Since this was a major issue that surfaced in many different situations, she made the following summary sheet for it:

I MUST BE STRONG AND NEVER SHOW WEAKNESS

Why This Is an Issue
Physically, my father was very strong. He rarely got sick and had a high level of energy. He prided himself on his ability never to show any sign of weakness. Unfortunately, this also meant he almost never showed any sign of tenderness or empathy, since these were viewed as being signs of weakness. Because I wanted my father's love, I learned to be like him. Up until the assault, I've been able to pull this off fairly well.

Situations Where This Causes Problems
This issue has come up in a major way whenever my posttraumatic stress symptoms occur, and causes me to think that I have to return to my old position. If I don't, it will mean I'm weak. This core belief has also caused me to be overly critical when my two sons have shown weakness that is actually just a normal part of being young. Although I'm a good listener, I now realize that I've always prided myself at being stronger than most of the people I know. This has caused me to look down on others.

Things I Can Tell Myself
Although there are times when it is good to be strong, there are also times when it is OK to show weakness. I am not "superwoman." It's normal to hurt and have symptoms when traumatic real-life events occur. It's also normal and healthy to express sadness, pain, and fear. My father's need always to be strong poisoned all of his relationships. One of the ways he kept from showing emotions that he considered weak was to become angry and lash out whenever he was sad, hurt, or disappointed. It also caused him to pull away from people and fail to support those he loved when they needed him the most. There is nothing weak or demeaning about deciding to change jobs because I want a safer environment. It is healthy to want to avoid situations where you might be seriously hurt. When someone you love hurts, it's healthy and loving to comfort them. I do not need to "make them strong."

Things I Can Do
1. Keep quiet when my children make mistakes and encourage them.
2. Talk about some of the struggles I'm going through with appropriate people rather than always saying "I'm fine."
3. Read this sheet every day for a month.

As time went on, Kimberly found additional situations where the idea that she needed always to be strong interfered with her life. Each time she identified a new area, she added it to her summary sheet. Likewise, each time she thought of a new way to challenge this idea, she added that as well.

Two other incidents occurred in the months that followed that reactivated Kimberly's symptoms. The first occurred about six weeks after hearing about the employee who was hit with the coffee cup. Kimberly was driving in the country with her mother and children when a young man by the side of the road pointed a gun at her car as if he were going to shoot. While the young man was just pretending, Kimberly was so startled she drove off in a panic and her symptoms increased for about a week.

About three months after this, Kimberly was at a park with her two sons, her sister and brother-in-law, and their children when a group of young men who were obviously part of a local gang came to the park. Even though they were quite a distance away and did not bother Kimberly or her family, their presence was enough to trigger her symptoms again. This time, she experienced increased symptoms for about two weeks.

For each of the above incidents, Kimberly found that she needed first to go back and review her simple explanation and basic coping skills. She then went through her summary sheets so she could identify and address any additional issues that were playing a role in her increased symptoms.

The purpose in taking so much time with these examples is to impress on you two realities that are part of recovery. First, you will make relatively steady progress. Then something will happen that resensitizes you, triggering an increase in symptoms. Expect this as a normal part of the recovery process. Second, when this occurs, follow Kimberly's example and review all of the skills you are learning, beginning with the basics, and apply them in a systematic manner to whatever has triggered the increase in symptoms.

More Bumps along the Road to Long-Term Recovery

After working with Robert for seven months he reported that his desensitization was continuing to go well. His daily "jolts" of anxiety, as he described them, had stopped. He was eating in restaurants and working without excessive anxiety, and the only thing he still couldn't eat were chips. He had also flown on planes two times with no problems. We had reduced the frequency of our sessions to once every three weeks. Then, suddenly, he came in and reported that while he could still go anywhere he wanted without anxiety, his gagging response had returned and there was not a day when he wasn't thinking about choking. This new episode had been triggered when Robert inhaled some trail mix he was eating and panicked.

Like Kimberly, Robert was simply experiencing the normal ups and downs of recovery. He had gotten to a point in his recovery where he was using his tools consciously in only a small number of situations. During much of his day, he was no longer consumed with his symptoms. Now, because of the choking incident, his symptoms had again become a major focus. As with Kimberly, I had Robert simply return to the basics presented in chapters 5 through 8. Robert did this, and within three weeks he felt he was back on track.

After this incident, Robert continued to make steady progress for four months. Then another incident occurred. He was eating a steak and felt that something was stuck in his throat. He did not choke or have any real sign that there was a problem, only a "funny feeling." Nevertheless, that night, Robert was up until 2 A.M., worrying that something might be stuck in his throat. He also had a couple of brief episodes of gagging.

While these two episodes may look alike on the surface, there is an important difference. In the first episode, with the trail mix, there was a clear physical problem that produced a choking and gag response. In the second, as Robert described it, there was no physical obstruction that produced choking, just a "funny feeling" that he magnified. As Robert and I talked about what was going on in his life, he mentioned in a casual manner that he and his wife had an argument and were not getting along very well. When I pressed him on this issue, he admitted that the marriage was not good and added, "I'm just surviving."

The childhood message "Conflict is dangerous" was making it difficult for Robert to discuss or even think about issues that were important to him with his wife. In fact, he was "choking" on them. Issues difficult to deal with often cause symptoms that are symbolic, such as Robert's gagging. While Robert's symptoms are somewhat unusual, just like Mary's symptoms prior to her family get-together, they were functioning as a messenger. The message for Robert was "Tell your wife what is bothering you, and work out a solution."

D.E.R. Scripts

Like Mary, Robert needed to learn how to be more assertive so he would have more healthy boundaries. The only difference was that while Mary had weak boundaries that needed to be strengthened, Robert's boundaries were rigid and needed to be loosened. After presenting to him the concept of rights, as described in chapter 10, we moved on to a simple but powerful assertive skill that I call *D.E.R. scripts.*

The concept of D.E.R. scripts is easy to remember and an effective way of making your needs known to another. The letters represent the following:

Describe the problem.
Express your thoughts or feelings.
Request what you want.

The above elements are put together into a short three-to-five-sentence paragraph or script that you recite to the person with whom you are in conflict. It is important to phrase your sentences in what is commonly referred to as *I messages,* statements that tell the listener what *you* see, think, feel, or want in an objective manner that does not assign blame or put the listener down. (A statement that assigns blame or puts the listener down is often referred to as a *you message.*) Here is the script Robert developed to tell his wife what was bothering him:

> *Describe:* "Because I'm working a swing shift and you're working days, we don't spend much time together. The time we are spending together is mostly spent arguing about bills or things that need to be done."

> *Express:* "I'm feeling lonely and that you no longer care about me."

> *Request:* "I'd like to figure out a way where we can spend some quality time together and do something enjoyable."

The above script may look simple, but it took about thirty minutes to develop. The first and most difficult part of a D.E.R. script is identifying what you want, the "request" at the end of the script. When I first asked Robert what he wanted to change in his marriage, he listed a number of things that he wanted his wife to stop doing such as less arguing and less criticism. This is typical. But a good D.E.R. script focuses on what you want someone *to do* rather than on what you want stopped. I continued to pursue this with Robert. At first, because he was so used to focusing on problems rather than on solutions, he found it difficult to identify exactly what it was that he wanted. However, after some discussion, he realized that he wanted the companionship that was present when he had first met his wife.

Once you have clearly identified what you want, the rest is usually fairly easy. The only area where you need to exercise caution is in your description. The two basic rules for the description are (1) state just the facts and (2) keep it short. The purpose of the description is to present a problem that you are having in as succinct a manner as possible. The most common mistake people make is using "you messages" that involve negative labels or their "analysis" of the other person's motives or personality. Here is an example of a poor description that has both of these mistakes:

> Since I've been working the swing shift you seem to be
> getting more and more unreasonable and going into
> your own little world. You never help with anything and
> you don't care about anything I'm involved with.

The above was actually Robert's first attempt at creating a D.E.R. script. Compare it with the one we eventually developed on page 182. Notice how Robert's first attempt is accusing and blaming. Had he said this to her, his spouse would probably have become defensive and begun to fight back. In contrast, the description that was eventually developed used "I messages" and invited Robert's spouse to participate in a problem-solving discussion.

Once you have made your request through a D.E.R. script, you need to be able to switch gears and listen to the other person. As you listen, try to identify that person's needs. Keep in mind that your goal is to find a way to meet both of your needs as much as is possible.

Using the D.E.R. approach, Robert was able to express himself effectively to his wife. During the following weeks, he was able to say the things he had been "choking back" and work out several issues that had been major sources of tension in his marriage. The result was that he and his wife were able to achieve a deeper level of intimacy and Robert's symptoms again subsided.

Honoring Your Responsibility to Respect the Rights of Others

In addition to developing the ability to use D.E.R. Scripts, Robert found work in two other areas helpful. The first was to develop an increased awareness of his responsibility to respect the rights of others. In essence, this is a mirror activity to the work Mary did to develop an increased sense of her rights. People with weak boundaries tend to be overly focused on their responsibilities. In contrast, people with rigid boundaries tend to be too focused on their own rights and fail to respect the rights of others. Here is a list of responsibilities that Robert worked with:

I have the responsibility to treat others with the same dignity and respect I desire from them.

I have the responsibility to allow others to decide what is best for them.

I have the responsibility to express my feelings and opinions in a way that does not insult or put others down.

I have the responsibility to allow others the right to refuse my request even though I might not like being refused.

I have the responsibility to listen to others and take them seriously.

I have the responsibility to accept the consequences of my mistakes without blaming others.

I have the responsibility to allow others their weaknesses without ridiculing or resenting them.

I have the responsibility of setting limits in a way that causes the least amount of harm to or pain in others.

Because conflict had become associated with danger during his childhood, Robert found it useful to create the following summary sheet that dealt with conflict.

CONFLICT IS DANGEROUS

Why This Is an Issue
I was physically and verbally abused as a child, causing conflict to became associated with pain.

OVERCOMING ANXIETY

Situations Where This Causes Problems
Whenever I'm in conflict with my wife or an authority figure such as my supervisor, I tend to withdraw or become
childlike.

Things I Can Tell Myself
Use the time tunnel idea:
1. State What's Happening: "I'm in the time tunnel. This
   situation is triggering feelings and responses from the past.
   They were appropriate when I was little. Now it's time to
   come back to the present."
2. State What's Real: "I am an adult. I am *not* a helpless little
   boy trapped at home anymore. I am an adult with rights,
   and adult skills and abilities. I'm not going to be beaten
   up. Use your adult abilities."

Things I Can Do
1. Take a few minutes to cool down when I'm angry.
2. Remind myself of my responsibilities.
3. Use my "time-out" to create a D.E.R. script.
4. If I'm sick, hungry, tired, or stressed out, delay discussing
   problems until I'm feeling better.

Summary of Key Ideas

1. There are many detours along the path to long-term recovery
   because the conditioned responses associated with anxiety-
   related problems usually become intertwined with core beliefs
   and associations from childhood.
2. Two things essential to overcoming avoidance patterns are regular practice and customizing your rational challenges to meet
   the specific lies that generate your negative self-talk.

3. It usually takes several cycles of forgetting what you've learned and going back through the basics before these skills and insights are internalized enough so they become automatic. Fortunately, relearning is usually easier than learning something for the first time.

4. As you recover, situations will occur that will trigger an increase in your symptoms. Expect this. When this happens, review the skills you are learning, beginning with the basics, and apply them in a systematic manner to whatever has triggered the increase in symptoms.

5. Issues that are difficult to deal with often cause symptoms that are symbolic, such as Robert's gagging.

6. D.E.R. scripts are an effective way to make your needs known to another.

7. When you create D.E.R. scripts, use "I messages," state the facts, and keep it simple. People with weak boundaries tend to be overly focused on their responsibility to respect the rights of others. In contrast, people with rigid boundaries tend to be too focused on their own rights.

8. If you tend to disregard the rights of others, take time to develop an increased awareness of your responsibility to respect their rights.

Recommended Activities

Continue Systematic Desensitization and Journal Keeping

There are several activities from previous chapters that need to be continued over a period of several weeks or months. The two most important are (1) practicing systematic desensitization and (2) using your journal to record your successes, develop rational challenges, and complete the various written exercises given in these activities. In addition, remember the "new car principle" and continue to review the summary sheets and the list of rights you created.

Practice Creating D.E.R. Scripts

While D.E.R. scripts might seem simple, it often takes quite a bit of practice before a person becomes skilled at creating them. During this week, identify at least three situations where you are in conflict with someone. Create a D.E.R. script for each situation. Write these scripts in your journal for future reference. If you find it especially difficult to create D.E.R. scripts, keep at it, developing several more until you have the hang of it. You can even consider past conflict situations and develop scripts that might have been used in them.

Continue to Work with Your Summary Sheets

Continue to create summary sheets for beliefs and associations that you identify as problems. Whenever you read or think of something new, add it to your sheets.

12

Two Important "Quiet" Messages

As a person moves along the path to long-term recovery, there are several quiet but essential messages that need to be heard. This chapter focuses on two that are often neglected, along with a systematic method you can use to hear more clearly the messages that anxiety brings.

Quiet Message One: Learn to Manage Periods of High Stress

Like most of my clients, Mary, Robert, and Kimberly had very poor stress management skills. A quiet but crucial message in their anxiety was that they needed to learn how to take care of themselves and manage stress more effectively. This is an important step on the road to long-term recovery. Here is how Robert took this step:

A few months after the trail mix episode described in chapter

11, Robert returned and reported that his symptoms had again returned. Since it was the first week in November, my first thought was that he might simply be having "holiday anxiety." However, as we talked, he reported that a number of highly stressful events were occurring at the same time. He was working on a swing shift from 4 P.M. to midnight as well as putting in lots of overtime because the deadline for a major project was rapidly approaching. To make matters worse, a routine audit of his unit was scheduled for the following week. Plus, he had sold a car to a friend that had been impounded in another city. Since his friend had not registered the car, it was still in Robert's name, making Robert responsible. In addition to the financial burden, he needed to make arrangements to go to this city during a weekday and clear up the matter.

This was clearly much more than just holiday anxiety. Robert was in a period of very high physical, mental, and emotional stress due to a number of events occurring at the same time. A simple idea to remember during times of excessive stress is that *your body has only a limited supply of energy.* By this I mean that you have only enough energy on a given day to do a certain number of things. On some days you can do more than on others. When you are experiencing lots of stress, as Robert was, the amount of energy you have is less than usual. Therefore, you need to use the energy you have wisely and take steps to replenish your energy for the future.

Two simple guidelines can help you conserve the energy you have. First, when under stress, set priorities and focus your attention on the most important issues. While this seems simple and logical, it is actually difficult to do because stress, especially when it's intense, reduces your ability to think clearly. This, in turn, causes you to think in more black-and-white terms, which often causes little things to become major issues. Take a moment to recall the last time you were experiencing high levels of stress. During this time you probably became very upset over many things that later proved to be unimportant. In order to curb this tendency, you need to remind yourself that you are experiencing unusual stress and to set priorities. Ask yourself, "What do I need to do that is truly important, and what can I put off?"

The second general guideline for periods of excessive stress is to take more time to make decisions. Since you are not able to think as clearly when under stress, you need to work through problems in a more deliberate and systematic way. When possible, delay making major decisions until you're experiencing less stress. Wait until you can think more clearly. If an important decision cannot be delayed, discuss your options with someone whose judgment you trust.

Robert applied these ideas to his situation and thought of a number of things he had planned to do around his house that could be put off for a couple of weeks. He also thought of several things at work that could be delayed until after the audit. In addition, since Thanksgiving was during the week following the audit, Robert decided to take a week's vacation after the audit and use this time to rest and rebuild his strength. While most people cannot take a week off like Robert, everyone can identify projects that can be delayed and use the time that is freed up to relax and reenergize.

Two Principles for Managing Everyday Stress

In addition to the guidelines for managing periods of high stress discussed above, there are two general principles for managing everyday stress. First, stay healthy. A strong, healthy body tolerates stress much more effectively than an unhealthy one. This is especially true for a person with a highly reactive body. You can increase your body's physical ability to tolerate stress by eating a well-balanced diet and exercising regularly. In addition to increasing your body's ability to carry stress, exercise also provides the benefit of helping you release tension and relax more completely.

Second, learn to pace yourself instead of rushing from one activity into another. Schedule short periods of time to unwind after stressful events. These "decompression" moments can range from short periods of ten or fifteen minutes to sit with a cool drink, chat with a friend, or do some other relaxing activity to longer periods where you do something relaxing and invigorating. Remember that a stressful event includes any period of intense physical, mental, or emotional activity, whether it is enjoyable or painful. Many of my clients forget that going to an enjoyable social event can be just as stressful for the body as attending an intense meeting at work or having an argument with a loved one.

Quiet Message Two: Find a Source of Spiritual Strength

The second quiet message, which is often ignored, is the need to have a source of spiritual strength. Because the spiritual realm is very personal, this is the most difficult area to explore with clients. This is especially true when deep wounds or conflicts have been experienced in this area. Because our culture often belittles or trivializes spirituality, many of us see the need for spiritual answers as unimportant. However, since we all must face death, illness, misfortune, and uncertainty, we all can use the comfort found in the spiritual realm.

What answers have you developed that can help you face death, illness, misfortune, and uncertainty? In Mary's case, she had been brought up in a traditional, mainstream church. However, like many, she had drifted away at an early age. After discussing the need for a spiritual connection, Mary decided to visit several churches near her. After about a month she found one that felt comfortable and was soon deriving much solace from this reawaking of her spiritual side.

In Robert's case, neither of his parents belonged to a church and they were both openly hostile toward religion. Because of this, Robert was suspicious of anything associated with formal theology. I encouraged Robert to go to the bookstore and browse through the religious and self-help sections and buy a book dealing with some aspect of spirituality that appealed to him. He found books dealing with the problems of life from a philosophical perspective most appealing. He liked the idea of meditating, and began to explore this discipline. Taking time to center himself each day became an integral part of his healing.

Unlike Mary, Kimberly did not stop attending church when she became an adult, and considered herself fairly spiritual. Unfortunately, she had been so focused on finding psychological answers to her posttraumatic stress disorder that she had not considered the problems from a spiritual perspective. It's common for people to separate their spiritual life from their everyday secular life. With my encouragement, Kimberly began to consider what had happened and the symptoms she was experiencing in a more spiritual context. Since she had made little formal study of her church's views, she found it helpful to discuss what she was going through with members of her church who were mature in their faith. The result was that she found her spiritual life to be a tremendous source of comfort and strength.

There is no way I can give you a simple recipe for how you can find comforting answers to the spiritual questions posed at the beginning of this section. However, I have found that once a person becomes aware of the importance of spirituality and begins to explore it, they find what they need. While this usually takes time and searching, the effort is greatly rewarded.

If you already have a source of spiritual comfort, simply begin to integrate it with the work you are doing in this book. This integration needs to be in two different areas. First, think about how your beliefs about God, the spiritual realm, death, and misfortune can be used to strengthen your rational challenges and coping self-statements. Second, if you have a method of prayer, meditation, or quiet time that you've practiced in the past with good results, begin using it on a daily basis. If you've never tried any of these, consider trying one for a period of at least a month. It's amazing how a short period of prayer, meditation, or quiet time over several weeks can speed up the healing process and help you see yourself and others more clearly.

Developing a Message Checklist

One of the central themes of this book is that anxiety is a messenger. One way to learn how to hear the message of anxiety is to develop a checklist of possible messages. The model of needs presented in chapter 4 provides a simple framework for doing this. Here are the four categories that were discussed in that chapter:

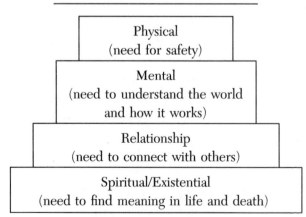

FOUR BASIC CATEGORIES OF NEEDS

Physical
(need for safety)

Mental
(need to understand the world
and how it works)

Relationship
(need to connect with others)

Spiritual/Existential
(need to find meaning in life and death)

When anxiety occurs for no apparent reason, take a quick inventory of your current situation in respect to these four categories. You can ask yourself the following questions to explore each category:

1. Physical (need for safety)

   - Am I sick, hungry, or tired? (It's surprising how often anxiety is simply telling you that you are doing too much and need to take better care of yourself.)
   - Have I taken on more things than I should?
   - Have I spent more than I should?
   - Is my job secure?
   - Is my home secure?

2. Mental (need to understand the world and how it works)

   - How am I feeling about myself at this stage of my life?
   - Is there a problem in how I'm fulfilling my roles as a man/woman, husband/wife, father/mother, son/daughter, or friend?

3. Relationship (need to connect with others)

   - How are my relationships going?
   - Am I lonely?
   - Am I in conflict with anyone?
   - Has anyone said or done anything hurtful recently?
   - Do I need to make amends for something I have said or done?
   - Has a friend or family member moved away?
   - Do I feel that I have at least one intimate relationship? (This refers to emotional *not* sexual intimacy.)

- Do I have at least one person I can talk to about the things that concern me without fear of being criticized or shamed?

4. Spiritual/Existential (need to find meaning in life and death)

- How am I feeling about my current situation in life?
- Do I have a sense of purpose in my life?
- Has anyone close to me died or been seriously ill?
- Has anything important happened that reminds me of my mortality and inability to control events?
- Am I taking care of myself physically, spiritually, and emotionally?

As you gain more experience in hearing the message of anxiety, you will find that simply asking yourself, "What is the message?" will immediately make you aware of something you've been ignoring. Until then, use the above questions to stimulate your thinking.

Summary of Key Ideas

1. Learning to take care of yourself and manage stress more effectively is an important step on the road to long-term recovery.
2. Your body has only a limited supply of energy.
3. During times of excessive stress you need to set priorities and focus your attention on the most important issues, and take more time with decisions.
4. You can manage everyday stress more effectively by increasing your body's physical ability to tolerate stress through exercise and a well-balanced diet, and learning to pace yourself by using short "decompression" periods after stressful activities.

5. Developing a source of spiritual strength is often an essential part of the healing process.
6. A short period of prayer, meditation, or quiet time can speed up the healing process and help you see yourself and others more clearly.
7. When anxiety occurs for no apparent reason, use the "message checklist" on pages 194–96 to identify the message your anxiety is sending you.

Recommended Activities

Dedicate a Short Period of Time Each Day to Study

At this point, many people feel overwhelmed by the many different areas they need to address in order to achieve long-term recovery. While there is a lot to do, don't feel that you must do everything at once. A short study period—ten to twenty minutes—five days a week is sufficient.

Choose a time when you will not be disturbed and that can be a regular part of your schedule, such as after breakfast, during a lunch break, after dinner, or before you go to sleep. Begin by reviewing the section of the book and the summary sheet on which you're currently working. Use the remaining time to rotate through the various activities you have identified as important for you. For example, you might spend three or four days working on D.E.R. scripts, then several days reviewing and adding to your summary sheets. After that, you might spend several days reviewing another area that you have identified as a core issue that still needs work. Use your journal for this work. Writing is a powerful way to analyze issues more objectively and to internalize new ideas.

When you come to a "detour," develop a summary sheet that addresses it. Be sure to keep the summary sheets you create for at least six months as you will probably need to refer to them when this issue recurs. When it does, don't get discouraged. Remember that it's just part of the normal learning process. Core issues from childhood need to be addressed many times before you've internalized the concepts and behaviors you need to conquer them.

Develop Skills for Managing Periods of High Stress

This chapter introduces the idea that the body has a limited supply of energy. It then offers two general guidelines for managing periods of high stress effectively: First, set priorities and do only what is most important. Second, take more time with decisions, delaying important decisions when possible.

Take ten to fifteen minutes to think about times when you have experienced excessive stress in the past and how you might have applied these principles to those situations. Then, think about times in the next few months when you will be experiencing increased stress and identify how you might apply these principles to those situations.

Learn to Pace Yourself

Take time this week to consider how you schedule your days. Identify ways in which you can pace yourself more effectively. Be sure to include short decompression periods between stressful activities. Keep in mind that anything that requires mental concentration or physical activity uses your energy. Take short breaks throughout the day to allow your body to recharge. It will help you manage both your stress and your work more effectively.

Take a Look at Diet and Exercise

This chapter discusses how you can increase your body's physical ability to tolerate stress through exercise and a well-balanced diet. Take time this week to consider what you have been eating. If you are not sure what constitutes a well-balanced diet, read a book on nutrition. In general, stay away from fad diets, and eat well-balanced meals based on sound nutritional principles. If you have any medical problems, consult your physician before modifying your diet.

If you are not exercising regularly, find a form of exercise you can do for at least twenty minutes at least three times a week. Choose something that matches your personality and way of life. If you have any medical conditions, be sure to consult your physician. If you've never exercised routinely, you may be surprised how regular exercise can reduce anxiety and increase your ability to tolerate stress.

Use the Message Checklist to Identify the Message of Anxiety

Start using the message checklist introduced on page 194 whenever you experience anxiety for no apparent reason. Be sure to record your discoveries in your journal, so you have a record you can review when anxiety recurs. You may be surprised at how often the answer to current anxiety is something you've already worked through but forgotten.

If you do find that you are quickly forgetting important realizations and slipping into old patterns, don't be discouraged. This is normal and part of how a person heals from emotional wounds that are deep and that have been present for many years. With time, you will find it easier and easier to remember your insights and apply them to the skills you are learning. Eventually, those skills will become as automatic as your old behaviors. Creating summary sheets can help to speed up this process.

13

Viewing Yourself in a New Way

Your Self-Image

In addition to the other areas that have been discussed in previous chapters, Mary, Robert, Kimberly, and most of my clients find work in the realm of self-image an important part of their long-term recovery. Your *self-image* includes all of the beliefs you hold about your strengths and abilities, your weaknesses and short-comings, as well as the personality traits you use to distinguish yourself from others. In essence, it is the picture you have of who you are.

One aspect of self-image that receives much discussion in self-help books is *self-esteem*. Self-esteem refers to the value you place on yourself, and it is reflected in the amount of respect you give yourself. People with a high level of self-esteem see themselves and their needs as important; they acknowledge their needs and take steps to meet them in a positive manner, stand up for their rights, and treat themselves with respect. The respect they have for themselves tends to be reflected in their view of others, giving them a greater capacity for love.

Many books on this topic mistakenly talk about self-esteem in isolation from *self-image*. In fact, your level of self-esteem is directly dependent upon your overall self-image. It is impossible to have a high level of self-esteem if you see yourself as incompetent, inferior to others, or unlovable. If you try to boost the level of your self-esteem but have important areas where you view yourself negatively, your efforts will be ineffective or the results short-lived. Conversely, if you are able to develop a more positive self-image, you automatically will have a higher level of self-esteem.

There are two general approaches for developing a more positive self-image: First, challenge negative core beliefs that developed during childhood whenever you notice them influencing your thinking. For example, the main negative core beliefs Mary had to challenge were "I'm inferior to others" and "I'm not as intelligent or capable as others."

Second, identify habit patterns associated with negative core beliefs and practice replacing them with behaviors that reflect positive beliefs. For example, it's common for people with a poor self-image to criticize themselves and use negative labels to describe themselves. In Mary's case, she often said things such as "That was so stupid of me, I just never do anything right." When we talked about this, Mary recalled that this was an expression her mother frequently used when Mary was young and made the mistakes typical of children.

As you identify negative labels that you use with yourself, develop more positive replacements. Mary decided that whenever she caught herself repeating her mother's words, she would say, "No. I am not stupid. Those are my mother's words and they're not true. I do many things well and have a good head on my shoulders. I just made a mistake that is no different from the mistakes that others make."

Mary recorded her ideas on the following summary sheet. She reviewed it regularly for several weeks and found that it helped her recognize those times when she was being influenced by these negative core beliefs. It also helped her remember what to do to change them. As she continued to challenge these old beliefs and substitute her new behaviors, Mary found that she began feeling more and more at ease in social situations. She also found that she was becoming less critical of herself.

CHALLENGING THE LIE THAT I'M INFERIOR TO OTHERS/I'M NOT AS INTELLIGENT OR CAPABLE AS OTHERS

Why This Is an Issue
I was teased a lot by my brothers when I was young. They constantly called me stupid and laughed at my ideas. They knew more than me because they were older, but I thought it was because I was stupid. Mom also tended to make negative comments and treat me as though I were incompetent. I think that one of the reasons she did this was because she saw herself as being stupid and incompetent. Mom was also over-protective. She never let me do anything "dangerous" or "unladylike."

Situations Where This Creates Problems
1. Whenever I make a mistake I call myself names like "stupid" and ridicule myself.
2. I worry a lot about people noticing my mistakes and thinking I'm incompetent. Even when I'm doing things that I'm good at, I act as if I'll be found out and people will see that it's not really true.
3. I tend to "freeze" whenever I'm asked to give an opinion or I need to make a decision about something.

4. I apologize a lot when I give an opinion, and I belittle my own ideas.

Things I Can Tell Myself
I may not be a genius, but I'm not stupid either. I'm normal and that is all I need to be. I have many strong qualities and abilities. I'm a good cook, I do more work than most at the office, people like to talk to me, I care about others, I am able to help others with their problems and I often see possibilities that others can't see. My boss and co-workers also see me as being quite clever.

Use the time tunnel idea:
1. *State What's Happening:* I've gone into the time tunnel and feel like a little girl trying to compete with my older brothers who are waiting for the chance to put me down. Come back to the present.
2. *State What's Real:* I am not stupid or incompetent. I am a valued employee at work and have made lots of excellent decisions. In fact, I out-produce most of my co-workers and make fewer mistakes. I simply believed a lie when I was young.

Things I Can Do
1. Whenever I notice that I'm putting myself down or using negative labels, I can immediately tell myself the truth and use more positive labels.
2. I can take a few moments to recall the many things I do well and how I've succeeded at many things.
3. I can stop comparing myself to others. When I catch myself doing this, I can remind myself that there will always be people more skilled as well as less skilled at whatever I choose to consider. It doesn't matter because I'm not in a race with anyone. No one is keeping score on how I do.

4. When someone gives me a compliment, just say, "Thank you."
5. I do not need to apologize when I give an opinion. Simply state it. Do not add things like "This probably isn't very good . . ."
6. When asked for my opinion, if I get anxious say, "Let me think about this for a moment." Slowing things down removes the time pressure I feel and helps me think more clearly.

What Makes Me Valuable?

One area of belief people often overlook when considering their self-image is their answer to the question "What makes a person valuable?" Everyone has absorbed from their family and the culture in which they were raised a set of beliefs about what gives value to a person. However, most of my clients have never thought about this consciously.

Chapter 9 describes Kimberly's struggle to accept that she was a normal person who had experienced an abnormal situation. This was actually the first step in changing her self-image. Chapter 11 described her efforts to challenge the core belief that she always had to be strong and never show weakness. While Kimberly was growing up, her father's scorn of weakness and his praise of her whenever she was strong taught her that being strong was a trait that gave a person value. Her summary sheet (shown in chapter 11) became her first step in dealing with the issue of what made her valuable.

Kimberly's belief that one has value when being strong is only a variation on the general theme that you only have worth when you do something valuable. This idea comes from several sources. In our culture, athletes, actors, politicians, and others who succeed are rewarded with money and praise. In movies and television programs, the person who is the strongest, most clever, or most successful is often cast as the hero. Even heroes who are inept redeem themselves by doing something wonderful. Clearly, our culture places a tremendous value on achievement and looks down on those who fail.

In addition to the cultural messages, Mary, Robert, and Kimberly also received this message from their parents. All three were raised in homes where there was at least one parent who constantly criticized their efforts. They only received approval from this parent when they performed in a manner deemed acceptable by the parent. This gave the message that they had value and were worthy of love only if they performed correctly. When a parent, like Kimberly's father, is a perfectionist and demanding, it amplifies this message.

One of the tasks that Mary, Robert, Kimberly—and most of my clients—find important is to make conscious decisions about what gives them value. This task returns us to the realm of spiritual beliefs.

In chapter 12, Mary and Kimberly both found the answers to their spiritual needs in their churches, while Robert took a philosophical approach. Because Robert was having difficulty in defining what he believed, he struggled the most with this task. However, after much thought, he began to develop rational challenges that were satisfying for him. Here is the summary sheet that Robert developed.

WHAT MAKES ME VALUABLE?

Why This Is an Issue
My parents were very critical and put me down a lot when I was young. Because of this I came to believe that I was worthless and would only be seen as valuable if I did something worthwhile. This is a lie.

Ideas I Can Use to See Myself as Valuable
That I exist is important apart from how I feel or what I do. My value as a person is a separate issue from the value of the activities I do. Equating worth with achievement is an arbitrary value system for which there is no objective support. I am a human being who does various activities. I am not those activities. While my activities may or may not be valuable, they do not add or subtract from my value as a person.

How I live is more important than what I do. Enjoy the "doing" and the destination will take care of itself. The journey is more important than the destination.

I work to improve myself because of the joy and fulfillment it brings—not because it will somehow make me a better person.

In order to have healthy, satisfying long-term relationships, who I am as a person is far more important than what I do.

At the end of my life, the lives that I've touched and the relationships I've enjoyed will be more important than the things I've done.

The summary sheets Mary and Kimberly developed were very different from Robert's, as they focused on answers that came from their faith. Since Mary's and Kimberly's summary sheets were similar, only Mary's is included.

WHAT MAKES ME VALUABLE?

Why This Is an Issue
My brothers were constantly putting me down and making fun of everything I did. My parents did little to stop this and offered me little encouragement of their own. Because of this I came to believe that I couldn't do anything correctly and was inferior to others. This caused me to see myself as having no value. This is *not* true. I am just as valuable and capable as anyone else.

Ideas I Can Use to See Myself as Valuable
I am a creation of God. He values me. Indeed, here is how God sees me: "What is man that you are mindful of him, the son of man that you care for him? You made him a little lower than the heavenly beings and crowned him with glory and honor. You made him ruler over the works of your hands; you put everything under his feet: all flocks and herds, and the beasts of the field, the birds of the air, and the fish of the sea, all that swim the paths of the seas. O LORD, our Lord, how majestic is your name in all the earth!" (Psalms 8:4–9)

"Don't you know that you yourselves are God's temple and that God's Spirit lives in you? If anyone destroys God's temple, God will destroy him; for God's temple is sacred, and you are that temple." (1 Cor. 3:16)

God values who I am much more than what I do. Remember the Beatitudes (Matt. 5:3–10).

This is what God values:
The parable about the rich man who was consumed with

---

acquiring wealth reflects God's views about material wealth: "But God said to him, 'You fool! This very night your life will be demanded from you. Then who will get what you have prepared for yourself?' This is how it will be with anyone who stores up things for himself but is not rich toward God." (Luke 12:20–21)

Notice how Mary used Bible verses that were important to her. I have found it useful for clients with strong religious ties— whether they are Christians, Jews, Buddhists, Moslems, or any other faith that has a sacred text—to incorporate key verses from their scripture into their rational challenges. If a person practices daily prayer or meditation, I also encourage them to devote a small portion of this time to wrestling with the lies from childhood that still haunt them.

Notice that sections of Robert's and Mary's summary sheets are simply different ways of saying the same thing. As you create your own summary sheets, keep in mind that you are the only one who is going to read them. Put down anything that helps you challenge the lies that have held you captive since childhood. Make your summary sheet a living, working document that grows and develops as your understanding of yourself and the world evolves.

Perfectionism

Perfectionism is a trait that affects how you view yourself and is common to those suffering from severe anxiety. It is the tendency to be displeased with anything that is not perfect or does not meet extremely high standards, and it is driven by the belief that perfection is possible. Another contributing factor is the tendency to exaggerate the importance of common, everyday mistakes. Associating your value with achievement also promotes perfectionism. Since I've already discussed the need to redefine what makes you valuable, this section will focus on the beliefs that "perfection is possible" and "mistakes are terrible."

Mary, Robert, and Kimberly were all raised by parents who were themselves perfectionists. Robert's and Kimberly's parents were much more extreme than Mary's, so their struggle with perfectionism was more difficult than hers. While I worked with all three, the first step was to identify times when perfectionism was a hidden source of increased symptoms or inappropriate behavior. The next step was to create statements that challenged perfectionistic thinking and to identify new behaviors that could be substituted for old ones. Here is the summary sheet Robert created to challenge the idea that perfection is possible.

PERFECTIONISM: PERFECTION IS IMPOSSIBLE TO ACHIEVE

Why This Is an Issue
My dad and mother were both very critical. It was rare when they said I did something correctly. I grew up knowing that my parents would only accept perfection. Anything less was met with ridicule.

Situations Where This Causes Problems
1. At dinners, work, and in other social situations, I seem to look for things to complain about. The thing I need to focus on is when I start complaining about something.
2. In situations where I've made a mistake of some kind, I go on and on about how awful it is.

---

3. In situations where I don't understand something, whether it is something simple like a business form or the behavior of someone, I go on and on about what should happen.

Things I Can Tell Myself
Perfection is by definition impossible to achieve. Humans never do anything perfectly. There is always room for improvement. If my goal is perfection, I've guaranteed failure. Remember that perfection is a direction, not a place.

Things I Can Do
1. Take time to focus on the positive aspects of what I have done instead of dwelling on what's wrong.
2. When I catch myself nit-picking, use the above ideas.
3. Practice seeing what's positive in the things others do and say less about what is wrong.
4. Practice giving compliments and building others up. Become an encourager rather than a discourager.

Mistakes Are Terrible

Perfectionism probably generates the most problems when it causes a person to exaggerate the importance of mistakes. A person can become so focused on the fact they made an error, they fail to seek a solution in a logical, step-by-step manner. Both Mary and Robert found this was especially true for them. In developing an approach to address this problem, they needed to address two issues.

First, they needed to develop self-talk that helped them to stop focusing on the problem and begin to focus on the solution. Then, they needed to learn to use a systematic approach for solving the many problems that mistakes create. Here is the summary sheet

Robert developed for mistakes. Since this was related to the issue of perfectionism, he kept these two sheets together.

PERFECTIONISM: CHALLENGING THE LIE THAT ALL MISTAKES ARE TERRIBLE

Why This Is an Issue

It was rare when my parent's said I did something correctly. Most of the time they would go straight to some little thing that wasn't perfect and dwell on it. These were things that were usually normal for a child my age. In school, I had a hard time, and the kids and teachers often made fun of me. I became terrified of making a mistake because of the pain and embarrassment it caused.

Situations Where This Creates Problems

1. The biggest warning sign is when I go on and on about how terrible a mistake is or how stupid I am for making it.
2. I usually become very angry
3. I begin to act like my parents. I blame others for my mistakes and say hurtful things that are not true.

Things I Can Tell Myself

1. Remember that making a mistake or failing at a task doesn't make me a failure. My worth as a person has nothing to do with what I do. "Because I made a mistake doesn't mean I am one" (Hugh Prather).
2. The truth is that most mistakes are unimportant. They happen all the time. Is this error going to be a major life-changing event? Will it be important a week or a month from now?
3. Mistakes are a natural part of the learning process. Mistakes are gifts of wisdom.

---

4. Quit focusing on how terrible the mistake was and use the three-step problem-solving approach.

Things I Can Do—Use the Three-Step Problem-Solving Approach
1. What happened?
2. Can it be corrected? If so, how? If not, move on.
3. What have I learned from this? Is there any way I can avoid making this mistake in the future? Keep in mind that there are some things that you can't prepare for or prevent.

Learning to Become Friends with Your Emotions

Emotions simply send the message that a need either must be addressed or has been met. Sometimes this need is a difficult life event, such as illness or misfortune; other times, it is a reminder of unhealthy core beliefs, conflicts in relationships, or unresolved spiritual issues. The most difficult lesson for most of my clients, including Mary, Robert, and Kimberly, is for them to accept and become friendly with their emotions, that is, to view their emotions as part of being a healthy, normal human being. As they become more acceptable, emotions become more manageable. You will find that their intensity no longer frightens you.

It may be that you experience some or many emotions more intensely than most people. This is common for people who are sensitive. This does not make you weird or abnormal, just different. The fact that you are sensitive is a *normal* variation, one of the thousands of ways in which people are created and experience life. Always keep in mind that it is also a valuable asset that enables you to experience more joy and understand things and people more clearly than the average person.

Unexpected Anger

One of the emotions that Mary had to befriend was anger. After three weeks of reviewing the list of rights described in chapter 10 and using the D.E.R. scripts described in chapter 11, Mary began to experience levels of anger that were uncharacteristic and that frightened her. She had always prided herself in the fact that she only rarely became angry. Now she was not only feeling much more anger, but, on a few occasions, was showing that anger to others. This is a common experience. When someone who has avoided conflict, suppressed anger, and acted nonassertively begins to be aware of personal needs and acts assertively, he or she often finds anger appearing more frequently.

Chapter 4 points out that anger and fear are the two possible emotional responses we have when a need is threatened. Which one we experience depends on how we assess the nature of the threat and our ability to meet it. Chapter 4 also points out that anger generates energy and motivation to overcome the threat, while fear generates energy and motivation to avoid the threat. As a child, Mary ignored her needs and suppressed her anger in order to win her parents' approval. As a result, she had little experience with anger.

Since one of Mary's core beliefs was that she was unable to meet her needs, her usual response to the threat of unmet needs was anxiety or depression. (Her depression was due to the many losses she silently endured by not working to meet her needs.) Now, for the first time in her life, she was beginning to see that her needs were important and that she had the right and the ability to take steps to satisfy them. All of this meant that she was now assessing many situations as ones where she could overcome the threat that was present. This, in turn, triggered her anger. Because Mary had been suppressing anger for so many years, it took an elevated level of anger to break through that suppression and overcome her belief that anger was wrong. Just as she had been learning how to manage anxiety, she was now learning how to manage anger so that it could be her ally instead of her enemy.

After a few months of swinging back and forth between suppression and lashing out, Mary slowly found a middle ground: She began honoring the needs that were generating her anger while controlling her feelings in a way that was appropriate. While this initial experience of anger is often distressing for someone like Mary, it usually doesn't take too long for the person to become comfortable with this "new" emotion and learn how to manage it effectively. This is an important skill, as low-level anger—usually labeled as irritation—provides the energy and motivation for assertive behavior.

Learning to "Normalize" Yourself

People with anxiety-related problems often feel alone and different from others. Frequently I hear them say they are "weird" and just want to be normal like everyone else. They often see others in an idealistic way, and as dealing with all of their problems effectively and going through life with ease.

One of the most difficult tasks on the road to long-term recovery is learning to accept yourself and everything you experience as simply normal variations of what humans experience. Core beliefs from childhood such as "I'm inferior," "I'm different," "I'm not lovable," and "I'm bad" make this acceptance difficult. I like to compare this dilemma to the old Groucho Marx quip "I wouldn't want to belong to any club that would have me as a member."

Likewise, most of my clients believe that anything associated with them cannot be healthy.

To illustrate the stance, I often joke with clients and say, "Did you know that talking to yourself is a sign of mental health?" I'll then ask them, "Do you know how I know this is true?" As they look at me with a perplexed expression, I say, "I know this because I talk to myself and I'm an expert on mental health." In a similar manner, you need to simply declare yourself normal. Part of being normal is having a few little quirks, which are no big deal. Look around. Notice the amazing variety of ways in which people are created and the amazing number of ways in which they adapt to and go through life. You probably view most of these differences as normal and *not* as signs of pathology. It's time for you to begin to view yourself in the same manner.

A common mistake that prevents people from seeing themselves as normal is confusing *normal* with *perfect*. Like Mary or Robert, those with a core belief that they are inferior in some way, often try to make up for it through perfectionism. If you can act "good enough" or do something "worthy," you can become acceptable. However, the unrealistic expectations associated with perfectionism cause you to see those actions and accomplishments as inadequate. This in turn reinforces the core belief that you are inferior.

Kimberly provides a good example of someone confusing normalcy with perfection. The unrealistic standards of her father taught Kimberly that only perfection was acceptable. This caused her to see her posttraumatic stress reaction as a major failure rather than as a normal response to an abnormal situation.

The force that drives the confusion of perfection with normalcy is the desire to be accepted by others. Mary, Robert, and Kimberly all had developed a core belief that others expected them to be perfect and that anything less would cause rejection. This false belief came from their childhood experiences of rejection by perfectionistic parents.

Redefining what is normal is one of the keys to achieving long-term recovery. A normal human is *not* perfect. Everyone has weaknesses and regularly makes mistakes. If you have a sensitive body you will experience more physical reactions to events than someone with a less sensitive body. Mary, Robert, and Kimberly were very tolerant of imperfection in others but had difficulty applying this view to themselves. As time passed, however, and they were able to see that *normal* does not mean *perfect,* they became more forgiving of their mistakes and temporary lapses into old patterns.

Summary of Key Ideas

1. Long-term recovery often requires the development of a more positive self-image.
2. Self-esteem is just a part of your overall self-image and refers to the value you place on yourself.
3. The two main approaches for developing a more positive self-image are (1) challenging negative core beliefs that developed during childhood and (2) identifying habit patterns associated with negative core beliefs and practicing new, opposite behaviors.
4. An important part of reworking your self-image is examining your beliefs about what makes you valuable.
5. Two lies that help maintain perfectionism are "Perfection is possible" and "Mistakes are terrible."
6. Learn to become friends with your emotions.
7. It's common for people who have suppressed anger to go through a process of learning how to experience anger and control it in healthy ways.
8. Learn to "normalize" yourself.

Recommended Activities

Develop Summary Sheets Dealing with the Topics in This Chapter

This chapter discussed several core issues that can be associated with severe anxiety. Develop summary sheets for any that apply to you. Be sure to include all four parts as discussed in chapter 10. In addition, take one or two days to review the summary sheets you prepared while working on previous chapters.

If you have not yet tried to create a summary sheet, I encourage you to do so now. It is a powerful tool.

Continue Desensitization and Keeping a Journal

Plan to continue working on these two key activities for several more months.

14

Final Steps

In the last few chapters, you've seen many of the ups and downs that Mary, Robert, and Kimberly went through as they moved toward long-term recovery. Although I've described the main detours each one took, I would have to add several more chapters in order to describe the additional detours that were variations of the ones already detailed. For example, chapter 11 describes two recurrences of Robert's gagging response. After these, there were two more incidents, several months apart. As with the episode where Robert needed to set limits with his wife, each of these two additional incidents was related to situations where Robert needed to speak up and set limits. One episode involved his work, and the other child custody issues with his first wife. Each time, we went through the same set of ideas described in chapter 11, and Robert was soon doing well again.

A year after our final session, I spoke with Robert and he reported that he had no further recurrence of the gagging response. He is now eating whatever he wants and has had no further excessive symptoms. This does not mean that he never experiences high levels of anxiety. Because of the nature of his work and who he is, Robert does occasionally experience some body symptoms, usually related to presentations and deadlines. However, he now sees these as a normal response to stressful situations. He uses his stress management skills and doesn't pay much attention to the anxiety he's experiencing. In fact, he has remarked that he now notices how his fellow workers respond during times of high stress and finds that he handles those times much better than they. As he so aptly put it, "I'm now an expert at how to handle stress."

During the year and a half that I worked with Mary, she also had several experiences that were similar to those described in previous chapters. Although it took her an additional year of desensitization on her own after we concluded our work together, she is also now able to run wherever she wishes and to travel freely. As with Robert, she finds that when she experiences intense anxiety, it is always related to stressful events. She is no longer frightened by anxiety and, like Robert, simply uses the skills she has learned to manage her anxiety and deal with the issues generating it.

Kimberly and I worked together for about a year. Unfortunately, during that time she also experienced several more every-day situations that triggered a recurrence of her posttraumatic stress symptoms. Toward the end of her therapy, she decided to go into a different line of work that required a move to a different city. About a year after our last session she sent me a letter. She was enjoying her new job and has had no further symptoms for many months.

Where Do I Go from Here?

One of the things I hope you have come to understand is that long-term recovery takes time. The more childhood issues that have become intertwined with your symptoms, the longer recovery will take. Because the message that anxiety is sending may be difficult to understand, you may need to retrace your steps. This is normal and part of the healing processes.

Since repetition is the key to success, I encourage you to read through this book again slowly and deliberately. Because the concepts and skills presented in the chapters are interconnected, it is easy to miss some or much of what is presented the first time you read them. Full mastery of a concept or skill presented in an earlier chapter often requires the mastery of concepts and skills presented in later chapters. Now that you have studied the ideas and practiced the skills in the later chapters, you have an increased ability to apply those that were presented in the earlier ones. Many will find that even working through the book a third time is very beneficial.

What If I'm Feeling Stuck?

It is common for many to find it difficult to work through a book such as this. If this is true for you, consider obtaining the audio cassettes described in the "Supplemental Materials" section at the end of the book. If you've been working on your own, you may decide to find a study partner or group of people who can help you stay motivated, and use the chapters as they are intended to be used.

If you're feeling really stuck, you might want to consider working with a therapist who is skilled with anxiety-related problems. A
good therapist can help you become aware of and work through
"blind spots" that you missed because they were associated with
especially painful issues. Use the guidelines for selecting a therapist given in appendix 2 to make sure you find someone who
specializes in anxiety-related problems.

Occasionally a client has a specific situation, place, or memory
that triggers an emotional response that is so strong, it overwhelms
the types of cognitive-behavioral techniques described in this
book. Examples would be an intersection where an accident
occurred, speaking with an especially threatening parent, or memories of a rape, mugging, or childhood trauma that produce excessively high levels of anxiety. When this is the case, I have found an
approach called eye movement desensitization and reprocessing
(EMDR) to be very useful. Other approaches, such as hypnosis or
Neural Linguistic Programming (NLP), can also help a person like
this. See appendix 2 for more information on finding practitioners
who use these types of approaches.

Applying Your Skills to Other Areas of Your Life

One of the things you'll find in the months ahead is that the skills
and insights you've gained are useful in many areas of your life
unrelated to anxiety. For example, as Robert moved into long-
term recovery, he began to realize that part of the dissatisfaction
he felt in his marriage came from his difficulty with intimacy. He
often felt distant from his wife and frequently spoiled good times
by starting fights with her over trivial matters. The force behind
this was the core belief "Intimacy is dangerous." Here is how
Robert applied the idea of summary sheets to this issue.

BECOMING FRIENDS WITH INTIMACY

Why This Is an Issue
My mother and father did not know how to be intimate in a positive way. Throughout my childhood we only connected in negative ways: put-downs, blaming, and fighting. For much of my life I've used these same ways to connect with others. Whenever I allowed myself to be vulnerable, I got stomped on.

Situations Where This Creates Problems
1. I pick on my wife and friends, pointing out negative habits and often putting them down.
2. I often act childish and make unreasonable demands.
3. I often experience irrational anger.
4. I often blame my wife for things that have nothing to do with her.

Things I Can Tell Myself
Use the time tunnel idea:
1. *State What's Happening:* I've gone into the time tunnel and become a child in my parents' home.
2. *State What's Real:* My wife is not my mother. I am not a child. I am an adult who is able to protect himself and be safe. My wife is capable of honest communication; my parents are not. My wife loves me and would not willingly do anything to hurt me. While my parents are not safe, my wife *is* safe. I can be vulnerable and intimate in positive ways with her.

Things I Can Do
1. Take a time-out. Leave the room where she is and take time to get out of the time tunnel by using the above rational self-talk.

2. Identify what I need. Three needs that often generate old family patterns are:

   a. I have had a disappointment or a hard day and simply need reassurance. Ask for a hug or time to sit with her.

   b. I have been hurt by something she has done. Keep in mind that this is often unintentional and she is often not aware that what she has done has hurt me.

   c. I need to ask for something that is difficult for me to talk about.

3. After I've identified what I need, construct a D.E.R. script and speak up. Be honest and direct. Remember my responsibilities and be kind.

Robert used the above summary sheet for several months. At first, he read it every day for three weeks. Then, each time an episode occurred where he repeated his old patterns, he would pull the sheet out and review it again. During our follow-up telephone conversation a year after his therapy ended, Robert reported that he still used this particular sheet every now and then. Although his struggle with intimacy continued, he had made much progress and his marriage was much more satisfying.

Many of my clients struggle with intimacy, safety, and conflict. If any of these is a problem for you, view it simply as another area of life where you need to go through a period of desensitization, as Robert did.

A Final Word

I encourage you to continue working toward the goal of long-term recovery. Many people have achieved this goal. You can as well.

Although the struggle may be the most difficult thing you do during your life, the growth, maturity, and strength you gain will be well worth the effort.

I would very much like to hear about your experiences as you worked through this book. Your comments and suggestions will help me tremendously when I make future revisions. Take a few minutes to write or type your answers to the following questions on a sheet of paper and send them to:

Reneau Peurifoy
c/o LifeSkills
P.O. Box 7915
Citrus Heights, CA 95621-7915

1. In general, what did you like about this book?
2. In general, what didn't you like about this book?
3. What chapter(s) or section(s) did you find most helpful? How?
4. What chapter(s) or section(s) did you find least helpful? Why?
5. What changes would you recommend for future versions of the book?
6. Do you have any other comments you would like to make about the book?

Appendix 1

The Main Types of Anxiety Disorders

Two common symptoms in anxiety-related problems are *panic attacks* and *agoraphobia*. These two symptoms can be described as follows:

Panic Attack
A panic attack is an episode of intense fear or discomfort in which four or more of the following symptoms develop quickly and reach a peak, usually within ten minutes or less.

- Palpitations, pounding heart, or accelerated heart rate
- Sweating
- Trembling or shaking
- Shortness of breath or sensations of smothering
- Feeling of choking
- Chest pain or discomfort
- Nausea or abdominal distress
- Feeling dizzy, unsteady, light-headed, or faint
- Derealization (feelings of unreality) or depersonalization (being detached from oneself)
- Fear of losing control or going crazy
- Fear of dying
- Paresthesia (numbness or tingling sensation)
- Chills or hot flushes

The Main Types of Anxiety Disorders

When a panic attack occurs out of the blue, it is called an *unexpected* or *uncued panic attack*. When a panic attack occurs in response to a specific situation, such as a large social gathering, or a specific cue, such as a bridge, it is called a *situationally bound* or *cued panic attack*. When a panic attack is likely to occur in response to a specific situation or cue but does not always occur in this situation, it is called a *situationally predisposed panic attack*. An example of someone with this would be a person who often has panic attacks while driving but sometimes drives the same route without experiencing a panic attack.

Agoraphobia

The key feature of agoraphobia is fear of being in places or situations from which escape might be difficult or embarrassing, or in which help may not be available in the event that a panic attack or severe anxiety occurs. This fear causes the person to avoid these types of situations, to endure them with marked anxiety, or to require the presence of a companion.

The Different Types of Anxiety Disorders

At this time, the main classification system that researchers and psychotherapists in the United States use for mental health–related problems is the fourth edition of the *Diagnostic and Statistical Manual of Mental Disorders* (DSM-IV), which was released in 1994. Below are the categories of anxiety disorders it lists:

Panic Disorder without Agoraphobia

In this condition a person has experienced unexpected panic attacks that have been followed by worry about having additional attacks and by the imagined dangers that such attacks might bring ("I might lose control," "I might go crazy," "I might have a heart attack," or "I might embarrass myself"). However, there is no agoraphobia present.

Panic Disorder with Agoraphobia
This condition is simply an extension of the previous one. In addition to having unexpected panic attacks and worry about symptoms, a person also has agoraphobia.

Agoraphobia without a History of Panic Disorder
Since over 95 percent of individuals who have agoraphobia also experience current panic attacks or have a history of panic attacks, agoraphobia without a history of panic disorder is fairly uncommon. One study found that the majority of the people diagnosed with this condition actually were found to have a specific phobia rather than agoraphobia when they were reevaluated.

Specific Phobia
A specific phobia is characterized by significant anxiety that is excessive or unreasonable and that is triggered by a specific situation or thing. In children, this anxiety can be expressed by crying, tantrums, freezing, or clinging. Adults with this condition usually recognize the excessive or unreasonable aspect of the anxiety. Within this diagnosis there are five subtypes:

Animal Type: Fear in this subtype is triggered by specific animals or insects. This type of specific phobia usually begins in childhood.

Natural Environment Type: Fear in this subtype is triggered by objects or events in the natural environment such as storms, heights, or water. As with the previous type, this usually begins in childhood.

The Main Types of Anxiety Disorders

Blood-Injection-Injury Type: Fear in this subtype is triggered by seeing blood or an injury or by receiving an injection or other invasive medical procedures.

Situational Type: Fear in this subtype is triggered by a specific situation such as being in or on public transportation, tunnels, bridges, elevators, planes, cars, or enclosed spaces. This type usually occurs either in childhood or in a person's mid-twenties.

Other Type: Fear in this subtype is triggered by situations or objects that do not fit into the above categories, such as the fear or avoidance of situations that might lead to choking, vomiting, or contracting an illness, or a child's fear of loud sounds or costumed characters.

Social Phobia
Social phobia is characterized by significant anxiety triggered by specific social or performance situations such as a social gathering, athletic or musical performance, or the delivery of an oral report in school or at a business meeting. These types of situations are either endured with high levels of anxiety or avoided. People with social phobia are usually concerned that they might embarrass themselves or that others will think poorly of them. For some people, just thinking about feared situations can produce severe anxiety and even panic attacks. People with this type of phobia usually recognize that their fear is excessive or unreasonable.

Obsessive-Compulsive Disorder
Obsessive-compulsive disorder, or OCD, is characterized by obsessions and compulsions that are severe enough to be time consuming (they take more than one hour a day) or cause marked distress or interference with a person's ability to function. An

obsession is a persistent idea, thought, image, or impulse that is senseless or repulsive and intrudes on a person's consciousness. Common obsessions involve thoughts of harming others, violating social norms by doing such things as swearing or exhibiting unacceptable sexual behavior, producing contamination or infection in oneself and others, and doubt about whether some action has been performed.

A compulsion is an action repeated in a ritualistic fashion. The action may be done with the intent to produce or prevent some future event or situation, even though the compulsion has no realistic bearing on the event or situation it is meant to affect. Compulsions can also be normal, rational activities performed in a clearly excessive manner. Compulsions are usually done in response to an obsession. For example, a person fearing contamination (the obsession) might engage in ritualistic or excessive hand washing. The most common compulsions are hand washing, counting, checking, and touching. Mild obsessions and compulsions are common and are considered a problem only when they interfere with normal activities, cause mental or emotional distress, or cannot be controlled by the person suffering from them.

Posttraumatic Stress Disorder
Posttraumatic stress disorder develops when a person has experienced, witnessed, or been confronted with an event or events that involved actual or threatened death or serious injury. This person reexperiences the event through distressing recollections, dreams, flashbacks, or heightened anxiety when exposed to situations or objects that resemble or symbolize the traumatic event. This person also tends to avoid things associated with the trauma and to experience a numbing, such as an inability to recall an important aspect of the trauma, diminished interest or participation in significant activities, and detachment or estrangement from others. Additional symptoms can include difficulty falling or staying

asleep, irritability, difficulty concentrating, hypervigilance, and an exaggerated startle response.

Acute Stress Disorder
This is simply a term used for a short form of posttraumatic stress disorder (PTSD). Acute stress disorder is diagnosed when the symptoms described in the previous section on PTSD occur within one month of a trauma and last at least two days but no longer than four weeks. If the symptoms last more than four weeks, the condition is then called posttraumatic stress disorder.

Generalized Anxiety Disorder
Generalized anxiety disorder (GAD) is a condition characterized by persistent and excessive anxiety and worry that lasts for at least six months. This worry is far out of proportion to the actual likelihood or impact of the feared event and tends to interfere with the person's ability to function. Although a person with this condition experiences symptoms characteristic of high anxiety, no panic attacks occur. Worries can include everyday, routine concerns such as job responsibilities, finances, the health of family members, or the safety of children. They can also include minor matters such as household chores, car repairs, or being late for appointments.

Anxiety Disorder Due to a General Medical Condition
This condition is characterized by anxiety resulting directly from a medical condition. Among the wide range of medical conditions that can cause anxiety symptoms are endocrine conditions (hyperthyroidism, hypothyroidism, pheochromocytoma, hypoglycemia, hyperadrenocorticism), cardiovascular conditions (congestive heart failure, pulmonary embolism, arrhythmia), respiratory conditions (chronic obstructive pulmonary disease, pneumonia), metabolic conditions (vitamin B_{12} deficiency, porphyria), and

neurological conditions (neoplasms, vestibular dysfunction, encephalitis).

In order to make this diagnosis, there must be evidence from the history, physical examination, or laboratory findings that there exists a general medical condition that can cause the symptoms. Sometimes this condition is characterized by anxiety or worry about a number of events or activities. Other times panic attacks, obsessions, or compulsions are present.

Substance-Induced Anxiety Disorder
This condition is characterized by anxiety, panic attacks, obsessions, or compulsions that are the direct result of a drug abuse, a medication, or a toxin.

Anxiety Disorder Not Otherwise Specified
This category is used for conditions where there is excessive anxiety or phobic avoidance but the overall picture does not fit any of the above categories. This category is most often a preliminary diagnosis given when there is inadequate or contradictory information. As more information is gathered, it is usually changed to one of the above diagnoses.

Appendix 2

Guidelines for Selecting a Therapist

A good match between a client and a therapist is required for successful therapy. The following guidelines are designed to help you find a therapist with whom you will have a positive experience and achieve the results you are seeking.

How Do I Start?

Begin by getting the names of at least three therapists. Start with people you know who either have been in therapy or might work with or know a therapist. You could also start by calling a therapist who has presented a class or lecture that you enjoyed.

If you have no personal contact with a therapist or someone who is familiar with therapists in your area, contact the Anxiety Disorders Association of America at 6000 Executive Boulevard, Suite 513, Rockville, MD 20852, (301) 231-9350. Ask for a listing of anxiety specialists in your area. Other possible sources of referrals include a family physician, a health insurance company, and medical schools, universities, or other major research and clinical centers. You could also look in the yellow pages of your local telephone directory under each of the following headings:

Psychologists: These are individuals who usually have a doctorate (Ph.D.) in psychology.

Appendix 2

Marriage and Family Therapists: These may also be called marriage, family, and child counselors. They usually have a masters (M.A. or M.S.) in counseling or psychology. Sometimes they have a doctorate (Ph.D.).

Social Workers: These are individuals with training similar to marriage and family therapists.

Psychiatrists: These are medical doctors (M.D.) who, after their basic training in medicine, specialize in psychiatry. Because psychiatrists are trained as medical doctors, they view anxiety as a medical problem and usually focus on determining which medication could be used to alleviate a person's symptoms. Since many psychiatrists work only with medication, you may need to go to one of the other types of therapists if you wish to use a nonmedication approach such as the one described in this book.

What Should I Ask?

After getting the names of at least three possible therapists, you need to interview each one to see if this is someone who specializes in working with your particular problem. Just as medical doctors specialize, therapists also have areas of specialty. Consider for a moment whom you would choose if you needed a specific type of surgery. You would get the best results from a surgeon who has performed the procedure hundreds of times. In a similar manner, you want to make sure you seek help from someone who has worked with many people with your problem. When interviewing a prospective therapist, the first step is to give them a short summary of your problem, describing your primary symptoms, how long you've had the symptoms, and the severity of them. Here is an example of what Mary might have said to a prospective therapist:

> I'm calling because I'm seeking a therapist who special-
> izes in anxiety disorders. I've been experiencing panic
> attacks for about five years. Currently I'm experiencing
> lots of anxiety and am unable to go more than a few
> miles from where I live, and I avoid lots of places like
> restaurants and theaters.

After you've given the prospective therapist a short summary of your condition, ask the following questions:

Are you licensed? (Many states do not license one or
more of the types of therapists listed on the preceding
pages)

*What kind of training have you had to work with my
type of problem?*

*How much experience have you had with this type of
problem?*

*How many people have you treated with this type of
problem in the past year?*

*What is your basic approach?/How would you work with
me?*

*What is your definition of success with my type of prob-
lem?*

How successful have you been?

How long does therapy usually take?

*How much does treatment cost and is any of it reimburs-
able by health insurance?*

Appendix 2

Which Approach Is Best?

There are many different therapeutic approaches, each with its own set of terms. With anxiety-related problems, it is best to find someone familiar both with cognitive therapy and with a form of behavioral treatment known as *in vivo exposure* (also called contextual therapy, travel therapy, or exposure therapy).

Cognitive therapy involves the learning of specific techniques for changing the way you think. Much of the material in this book is based on a cognitive approach, especially the discussion of distorted thinking in chapter 7 and the rational challenges in the later chapters. In vivo exposure uses as its primary tool progressive desensitization which is described in chapter 8. This approach concentrates on going into difficult situations and using specific behavioral and cognitive techniques to cope with the frightening feelings and thoughts as they occur. The "Situations Where This Creates Problems" and "Things I Can Do" sections of the summary sheets described in this book illustrate more sophisticated behavioral approaches.

Cognitive and behavioral approaches are often combined with other forms of treatment such as psychopharmacologic treatment (the use of medications) and psychodynamic therapy. The identification of core beliefs and associations that caused the development of symptoms is an example of a psychodynamic approach. Therapists who use a combination of these approaches usually tailor them to the needs of individual clients.

An exciting new approach I have found useful when combined with a cognitive-behavioral-psychodynamic approach is called eye movement desensitization and reprocessing, or EMDR. Unfortunately, it may be difficult to find someone who has adequate training in this method. Although EMDR seems deceptively simple, it actually requires a high degree of skill to use effectively. If you're interested in finding a therapist trained in this approach, write to or call:

EMDR Institute, Inc.
P.O. Box 51010
Pacific Grove, CA 93950-6010
(408) 372-3900

Since therapists often use the same terms in different ways *be sure to ask the therapist to explain what he or she means when a term you do not understand is used.*

How Do I Evaluate the Therapist Once I Start?

After two or three sessions, you need to decide if the therapist you've chosen has the knowledge, approach, personality, and style that seems right for you. Ask yourself the following questions:

Am I comfortable with my therapist?

Do I feel like I can speak freely with my therapist?

Does what the therapist say make sense and seem relevant to my problems?

Does the therapist speak in a way that is easy for me to understand?

Does the therapist take time to explain things I don't understand?

Does the therapist treat me as an adult rather than as a child or someone who is beneath him/her?

Do I feel comfortable disagreeing with the therapist?

Appendix 2

*Does the therapist take time to establish a set of goals for
my therapy that I can understand?*

It usually takes many months or years to achieve long-term recovery. This does not mean you spend all of this time going to weekly therapy sessions. Many people take periodic breaks from formal therapy to practice and master the skills they've learned. They then return when difficulties arise that they cannot resolve on their own. Others work weekly for an extended period of time. Though therapy often does take time, you should be able to see clear progress. *Do not allow your therapy to continue for months or years with no progress.* If you feel that you have made no progress and there is no clear direction to your therapy after six sessions, you probably need to try someone else.

Before you switch to a new therapist, tell your current therapist you are considering going to someone new because you feel your therapy is not going anywhere. It may be that you are simply not seeing the progress you are making. If you have tried several different therapists with little progress, you may need to reevaluate your efforts. Have you made a real commitment to the therapeutic process and done the work that you were asked to do? If not, return to the therapist who seemed most effective.

Appendix 3

How to Locate
Support Groups

The first place to look when trying to find a local self-help group is
the "Community Services" section of your telephone book. The
"Mental Health" subsection will list local agencies that can help
you find a self-help group in your area. If you have a local chapter
of the Mental Health Association, you will find this organization
especially helpful.

If you are unable to locate any agencies that know of local self-
help groups, the next step is to look in the yellow pages under
"mental health clinics," "psychiatrists," "psychologists," "marriage
and family counselors," and "social workers." As you look under
each heading, see if there are any clinics or therapists who specialize in anxiety-related problems. If there are, call them and ask if
they know of any local self-help groups.

After you have the names of several possible groups, it is time
to identify the one that is best for you. As with selecting a therapist, it is important to find a group that matches your needs. If
there are several chapters of a particular group in your area,
attend more than one so you get a flavor for each one. Attend at
least three meetings before deciding whether or not a particular
group is right for you.

If you are unable to locate a local self-help group, you may
want to consider forming one in your area. The Anxiety Disorders

Association of America can provide help in organizing a local self-help group. They can be contacted at:

Anxiety Disorders Association of America
6000 Executive Boulevard, Suite 513
Rockville, MD 20852
(301) 231-9350

A free packet of information on how to use this book with a self-help group is also available. To receive this packet, send $1.00 to cover the cost of postage and handling to the following address:

LifeSkills
Self-Help Group Packet
P.O. Box 7915
Citrus Heights, CA 95621

In addition to these resources from the ADAA, there are often many local resources available. If you have a local chapter of the Mental Health Association, you will find that they not only act as a great referral source but also train group leaders. I also recommend that self-help groups find a local therapist who is willing to serve as an advisor for the group. From time to time, the group will have difficulties that this person can help them solve. In my work as such an advisor I help the group to resolve the occasional personality conflicts that arise and provide the answers they cannot find in the books they use. Sometimes, when a person in the group realizes that the group is not an appropriate match, I help the group find other resources for that person.

As useful as self-help groups are, they do have limits. One is that they need to have a narrow focus to be effective. Many people with anxiety-related problems have nonanxiety-related issues that need to be addressed as part of their recovery. The three most common types of related issues are substance abuse, being raised in a dysfunctional family where physical, sexual, or emotional abuse occurred, and major illnesses or disabilities. When this is the case, an individual may find it helpful to attend one self-help group dealing with anxiety disorders as well as another group dealing with their other issue.

The *Self-Help Sourcebook* (see the "Recommended Reading" section for address) is another great national resource for identifying groups that deal with issues other than anxiety. It lists contacts and descriptions of more than four hundred national and demonstrational-model self-help groups along with extensive listings of self-help clearinghouses. I've found *The Self-Help Sourcebook* especially helpful for people who are trying to locate information on medical problems such as colitis or miner's disease. Physicians often do a very poor job at educating their patients, and the organizations listed in this directory can meet that need. For those thinking of starting a group, the directory also contains an excellent section on how to start an effective self-help group.

In closing, I would like to encourage professionals reading this to consider sponsoring a self-help group in their area if none exists already. If one or more already exist, offer your support as an advisor or resource person.

Appendix 4

How to Develop a Relaxation Response

Coined by Herbert Benson, the term *relaxation response* refers to a state of deep-muscle relaxation that is produced by some set method. Several common formal methods used by therapists to help a client develop a relaxation response include biofeedback, autogenic training, hypnosis, guided imagery, and meditation. This appendix gives brief descriptions of four popular methods you can use by yourself.

Set a goal of practicing fifteen to thirty minutes a day. All you need is a comfortable place to sit or lie where you won't be disturbed. It is also best to avoid using an alarm to signal the end of your practice session as this may startle you and cause your muscles to tense up.

Depending on which technique you use and how long you wish to spend, you can go through a particular procedure once, or you can combine them. For example, you could start with progressive relaxation, and then switch to Herbert Benson's relaxation-response technique.

If you find it difficult to use these approaches, consider purchasing one or more of the tapes listed in the "Supplemental Materials" section, or seek help from a local professional.

Progressive Relaxation

Developed by Edmund Jacobson in 1908 this procedure is the oldest of the "modern" methods for developing relaxation. It's based on the principle that your muscles become more relaxed after you tense them.

Close your eyes and notice how the various muscle groups and joints in your body feel. As you do this, note those areas that are most tense.

Beginning with the feet, tense and relax one muscle group at a time. As you slowly work your way up to your head and face, time the tensing and relaxing to your breathing. Breathing in a relaxed manner, tense as you inhale. Relax as you exhale. Be sure to use moderation as you tighten and relax each muscle group. Over-tightening of the toes or feet can cause muscle cramps. Excessive tightening of the neck and back muscles could result in a strain or injury.

Experiment with different muscle groups to find what works best for you. You might start by tightening and relaxing only the toes on the left foot and then the right foot. Or, you might find it best to combine muscle groups, such as tightening the toes on both feet at the same time.

After you've tensed and relaxed all of the muscle groups in your body, note how much more relaxed you are than when you began. Identify those areas where tension remains.

Breath Counting

In addition to being a good method for producing a relaxation response, this is an excellent focusing technique to use when you're having difficulty falling asleep.

Close your eyes and breathe in a normal, relaxed manner. Start with either fifty or a hundred and begin counting backward. Count each number as you exhale. There will be a slight pause between numbers. Use this time to notice how your body becomes still between each exhalation and inhalation.

As you count, use your imagination. Visualize the numbers as being three-dimensional or colored. You might even imagine pleasant sounds or music accompanying the appearance of each number.

It is normal for your mind to wander and for you to lose track of your counting. Each time this happens, simply resume counting from the last number you can remember.

Herbert Benson's Relaxation-Response Technique

Herbert Benson developed this technique after studying several different types of meditation. In this technique, a word or phrase serves as the center of focus. While any word can be used, three that are commonly chosen are *one, calm,* and *relax.* Some people prefer to use a short phrase such as "I am at peace," instead of a single word. You can also use words or phrases that have a spiritual or religious meaning such as "Shalom," "God is with me," or "I am being watched over."

Close your eyes and each time you exhale, repeat the word or phrase you have chosen as your center of focus. Adopt a passive attitude as you repeat your word or phrase. As with the other techniques, your mind will wander occasionally. When this happens, simply redirect your mind back to your word or phrase.

It is also helpful to use a secondary focal point in the form of a mental image that forms a background for the repetition of the word or phrase. For example, you might imagine a calm lake or a religious figure.

Fantasy

This approach is often referred to as imagery or visualization and is based on a simple principle: Anything you imagine vividly causes the corresponding physiological responses that would accompany the event in real life. You experience this principle whenever you watch a television program or movie. During scenes that are exciting, your muscles tense. During calm scenes they relax.

In essence, fantasy is simply "willful daydreaming." Close your eyes, breathe in a normal, relaxed manner, and imagine something peaceful and enjoyable. Since you want to produce relaxation, the only rule is to choose something that is peaceful and calming. Be as creative as you want. You can take an imaginary journey to the beach or mountains. You can recall a pleasant memory. This is your mind and your imagination, so you have complete control and can do anything you choose. If you are fairly tense, you may find it useful to use one of the previous techniques to calm yourself before you try fantasizing. If unpleasant thoughts occur, or if your mind wanders, simply redirect your mind back to your chosen fantasy.

Supplemental
Materials

This book has been designed to be used by itself. However, depending upon your personality and individual needs, you may want to consider obtaining one or more of the following supplemental materials:

The Relaxation Response Series

This series contains four programs on two audio-cassette tapes. These programs help you develop cue-controlled relaxation, the ability to trigger the relaxation response simply by placing the first two fingers and thumb of either hand together. These programs also help make relaxed diaphragmatic breathing, externalization, and basic stress-management skills automatic behaviors.

The Changing Attitudes Series

This series contains ten programs on five audio-cassette tapes. Designed to be used just before you go to sleep or while you practice deep relaxation, these programs communicate directly to your subconscious mind and focus on a wide range of issues such as distorted thinking, anger, assertiveness, and creating a positive self-image.

Overcoming Anxiety

On this set of seven audio-cassette tapes, the author of *Overcoming Anxiety* talks about the ideas and skills presented in each of the chapters of this book. You can listen to these conversations while you drive, work, or relax. This set of tapes is especially useful for people who find written material difficult to use and who learn best when information is explained verbally.

Taking Charge and Conquering Fear

On this set of eight audio-cassette tapes the author of *Overcoming Anxiety* talks about the ideas and skills presented in each of the chapters of his first book, *Anxiety, Phobias, and Panic.* Also included in this series are interviews with people who have used the program successfully.

The above materials can be ordered from:

LifeSkills
P.O. Box 7915
Citrus Heights, CA 95621-7915
1-800-4-Skills
1-800-475-4557

Recommended Reading

Self-Help Books on Anxiety

Beckfield, Denise. *Master Your Panic and Take Back Your Life!*

Bemis, Judith, and Amy Barrada. *Embracing the Fear.*

Bourne, Edmund J. *The Anxiety and Phobia Workbook.*

Burns, David D. *Intimate Connections.* (social phobia)

Clum, George A. *Coping with Panic: A Drug-Free Approach to Dealing with Anxiety Attacks.*

Foa, Edna B., and Reid Wilson. *Stop Obsessing! How to Overcome Your Obsessions and Compulsions.*

Markway, Barbara, et al. *Dying of Embarrassment: Help for Social Anxiety and Social Phobia.*

Neziroglu, Fugen, and Jose A. Yarya-Tobias. *Over and Over Again: Understanding Obsessive-Compulsive Disorder.*

Peurifoy, Reneau. *Anxiety, Phobias, and Panic: Taking Charge and Conquering Fear.*

Ross, Jerilyn. *Triumph over Fear.*

Recommended Reading

Schwartz, Jeffrey. *Brain Lock: Free Yourself from Obsessive-Compulsive Behavior: A Four-Step Self-Treatment to Change Your Brain Chemistry.*

Seagrave, Ann, and Faison Covington. *Free from Fears: New Help for Anxiety, Panic, and Agoraphobia.*

Williams, Karen. *How to Help Your Loved One Recover from Agoraphobia.*

Zimbardo, Philip. *Shyness: What It Is, What to Do about It.*

Books on Anxiety for Professionals

Barlow, David H. *Anxiety and Its Disorders: The Nature and Treatment of Anxiety and Panic.*

Beck, Aaron T., and Gary Emery. *Anxiety Disorders and Phobias: A Cognitive Perspective.*

Michelson, Larry, and L. Michael Ascher, eds. *Anxiety and Stress Disorders, Cognitive-Behavioral Assessment and Treatment.*

Ochberg, Frank M. *Post-Traumatic Therapy and Victims of Violence.*

Persons, Jacquline. *Cognitive Therapy in Practice.*

Shapiro, Francine. *EMDR: The Breakthrough Therapy for the Treatment of Trauma.*

———. *Eye Movement Desensitization and Reprocessing (EMDR): Basic Principles, Protocols, and Procedures.*

Walker, John R., G. Ron Norton, and Colin A. Ross. *Panic Disorder and Agoraphobia: A Comprehensive Guide for the Practitioner.*

Self-Help Resources

National Phobia Treatment Directory. Lists therapists working with anxiety-related problems throughout the United States. Call or write Anxiety Disorders Association of America, 6000

Recommended Reading

Executive Boulevard, Suite 513, Rockville, MD 20852, (301) 231-9350.

The Self-Help Sourcebook. Contains a listing of more than four hundred national and demonstrational self-help groups along with national toll-free help lines, and guidelines for starting a self-help group. Call or write: Self-Help Clearinghouse, Attn: Sourcebook, St. Clares-Riverside Medical Center, Pocono Road, Denville, New Jersey 07834, (201) 625-7101.

Additional Self-Help Books

Rational Thinking and Positive Self-Talk

Burns, David. *Feeling Good.*
————. *Intimate Connections: How to Get More Love in Your Life.*
Butler, Pamela E. *Talking to Yourself.*
Ellis, Albert, and Robert Harper. *A New Guide to Rational Living.*

Adults Who Were Physically, Sexually, or Mentally Abused as Children

Brown, Stephanie. *Safe Passages: Recovery for Adult Children of Alcoholics.* (physical, sexual, or mental abuse)
Davis, Laura, and Ellen Bass. *Allies in Healing: When the Person You Love Was Sexually Abused as a Child: A Support Book for Partners.*
————. *The Courage to Heal.*
Forward, Susan, and Craig Buck. *Betrayal of Innocence: Incest and Its Devastation.*

Recommended Reading

Miller, Alice. *Drama of the Gifted Child.* (emotional abuse, narcissism in parents)
Woititz, Janet Geringer. *Adult Children of Alcoholics.*

Substance Abuse

Black, Claudia. *It Will Never Happen to Me.* (for ACAs)
Gorski, Terence. *Passages through Recovery.*
Johnson, Vernon. *I'll Quit Tomorrow.*
Kinney, Jean, and Gwen Leaton. *Loosening the Grip.*
Milam, James, and Katherine Ketcham. *Under the Influence: A Guide to Myths and Realities of Alcoholism.*

Relationships with Substance Abusers

Beattie, Melody. *Co-Dependent No More.*
Drews, Toby Rice. *Getting Them Sober.*
Wegscheider, Sharon. *Another Chance: Hope and Health for the Alcoholic Family.*
Zink, Muriel. *Ways to Live More Comfortably with Your Alcoholic.*

Relaxation Techniques

Benson, Herbert. *The Relaxation Response* and *Beyond the Relaxation Response.*
Carrington, Patricia. *Freedom in Meditation.*
Davis, Martha, Elizabeth Robbins Eshelman, and Matthew McKay. *The Relaxation and Stress Reduction Workbook.*
Jacobson, Edmund. *Progressive Relaxation.*
Kabat, Zinn J. *Full Catastrophe Living.*
Le Shan, Laurence. *How to Meditate.*

Recommended Reading

Assertiveness

Alberti, R. E., and M. L. Emmons. *Your Perfect Right: A Guide to Assertive Behavior.*

Baer, Jean. *How to Be an Assertive (Not Aggressive) Woman in Life, in Love, and on the Job.*

Bower, S. A., and G. H. Bower. *Asserting Yourself: A Practical Guide for Positive Change.*

Smith, Manual. *When I Say No, I Feel Guilty.*

Marital Issues

Campbell, Susan M. *The Couple's Journey: Intimacy as a Path to Wholeness.*

Gray, John. *Mars and Venus in the Bedroom.*

————. *Men Are from Mars, Women Are from Venus.*

Hendriks, Harville. *Getting the Love You Want.*

Neil, Merrily, and Joanne Tangedahl. *A New Blueprint for Marriage.*

Rock, Maxine. *The Marriage Map: Understanding and Surviving the States of Marriage.*

Scarf, Maggie. *Intimate Partners: Patterns in Love and Marriage.*

Grief and Loss

Bozarth-Campbell, Alla. *Life Is Goodbye, Life Is Hello: Grieving Well through All Kinds of Loss.*

Kushner, Harold S. *When Bad Things Happen to Good People.*

Staudacher, Carol. *Beyond Grief: A Guide for Recovering from the Death of a Loved One.*

Viorst, Judith. *Necessary Losses.*

Recommended Reading

Books from a Christian Perspective

Allender, Dan B. *The Wounded Heart: Hope for Adult Victims of Sexual Abuse.*

Anderson, Neil. *The Bondage Breaker.* (sexual addiction)

Backus, William, and Marie Chapian. *Telling Yourself the Truth.*

Chapman, Gary. *Hope for the Separated.*

Cloud, H., and J. Townsend. *Boundaries: When to Say Yes and No.*

———. *False Assumptions: Relief from 12 "Christian" Beliefs That Can Drive You Crazy.*

Dobson, James. *Love Must Be Tough.*

Feldmeth, Joanne, and Midge W. Finley. *We Weep for Ourselves and Our Children: A Christian Guide for Survivors of Childhood Sexual Abuse*

Hart, Arch. *Children and Divorce.*

Hershey, Terry. *Beginning Again: Life after a Relationship Ends.*

Johnson, Laurene, and G. Rosenfeld. *Divorced Kids.*

Minirth, Frank, et al. *Love Hunger: Freedom from Food Addiction.*

Petersen, J. Allen. *The Myth of the Greener Grass.*

Richards, Larry. *Remarriage: A Healing Gift from God.*

Seamands, David. *Healing for Damaged Emotions.*

———. *Healing for Damaged Emotions: Workbook.*

Small, Dwight Harvey. *Remarriage and God's Renewing Grace.*

Smedes, Lewis. *Sex for Christians.*

Smoke, Jim. *Growing in Remarriage.*

———. *Growing through Divorce.*

———. *Living beyond Divorce.*

———. *Suddenly Single.*

Stoop, David. *Self-Talk: Key to Personal Growth.*

Townsend John. *Hiding from Love.*

Recommended Reading

White, John. *Eros Defiled.*
————. *Eros Redeemed.*

Other Topics

Covey, Stephen R. *Seven Habits of Highly Effective People.*
Frankl, Viktor. *Man's Search for Meaning.*
Fulghum, Robert. *All I Really Need to Know I Learned in Kinder-garten.*
————. *It Was on Fire When I Lay Down on It.*
————. *Uh Oh.*
Lakein, Alan. *How to Get Control of Your Time and Your Life.*
Lerner, Harriet G. *The Dance of Anger.*
Preston, John, Douglas Liebert, and Nicolette Varzos. *Every Session Counts.*
Prochaska, James, John Nareross, and Carlo Clemente. *Changing for Good.*

Index

accepting questionable sources
as authoritative, 111, 112
acute stress disorder, 231
advanced symptom control, 4,
140–43
agoraphobia, 227
agoraphobia without a history of
panic disorder, 228
all-or-nothing thinking, 105
anger, 49, 50, 214, 215, 217
anxiety
as a messenger, 2, 3, 5, 155,
156, 165, 181, 189
basic symptom management
skills, 87–102
developing a plan for stressful
events, 156, 157
drugs than can generate, 72
five factors that can trigger,
70–74
genetic predisposition, 4

holiday anxiety, 157
hormones and, 71
insight is not enough, 34, 40
limited supply of energy, 190,
196
managing rather than
eliminating, 3
medical conditions that can
generate, 72
message checklist, 194–96,
199, 200
need for repetition to
overcome, 150, 151, 171,
172
need for systematic work to
overcome, 6, 7
negative self-talk
characteristic of, 91–93
normal, 7, 125, 213–17
not dangerous, 92, 141–43

Index

anxiety *(cont.)*
  problems with current
    treatments, 1–3
  psychotherapy and, 10
  roadblocks to recovery, 170–
    72, 175–77
  sensitive body and, 70, 213,
    214
  setbacks, 155–59
  simple explanation for, 67–69,
    73–86
  stress and, 74
  symptoms of, 226, 227
  time to overcome, 8, 9, 141,
    150, 151, 153, 170, 171,
    219–21
  unconscious triggers, 34
  when stuck, 222, 223
anxiety disorder due to a
    general medical condition,
    231, 232
anxiety disorder not otherwise
    specified, 232
anxiety/panic cycle, 65, 66
approval, 214, 216
  value and, 205–9
approval, excessive need for,
    161–64
assertiveness, 159–61, 166–68,
    181–85

basic symptom control, 3, 4,
    139, 140, 149
biofeedback, 88
boundaries, 153–66
breath counting, 43, 45, 244

caffeine, 70, 72, 73
catastrophizing, 108, 115, 142
childhood abuse
  four common traits as adults,
    37–40
  holiday anxiety, 157
  reduced ability to understand
    events, 156
  spirituality and, 39
  suggestibility and, 135
  time tunneling and, 37
circular questioning, 105–8
cognitive psychology, 55, 236
conditioned responses, 32–35,
    40, 66, 140, 147, 149
confusion, 39
coping self-statements, 91–95,
    98, 101
  definition, 91
  incorporating sacred
    scripture, 207–9
  overcoming key stumbling
    blocks with, 141–47
core beliefs, 55–63, 170, 172,
    186
criticism, 162, 165
cue-controlled relaxation, 88,
    89, 99

decompression periods, 192
D.E.R. Scripts, 181–84, 187,
    188
  definition, 47, 57
  depression, 50
  desensitization. *See also*
    systematic desensitization,
    34

Index

diaphragmatic breathing, 89–91,
  99–101
discounting, 109, 115
dissociation, 39
distorted thinking, 103–119
  beliefs from childhood and,
    112, 114, 116
  definition, 104
  list of different types, 118,
    119
distraction. *See* externalization,
  96

early recollections, 16, 30
emotional reasoning, 109–13,
  116
emotions, 47–63
  behavior and, 50–51
  cognitive model of, 48, 57
  communication and, 50
  difficulty modulating, 38
  hard wired, 49, 51
  intimacy and, 223, 224
  learning to become friends
    with, 213, 214
  needs, 52–55, 57
  process that generates, 48, 49
  why we have, 49–52
existential needs. *See*
  spirituality, 53
externalization, 96–98
eye movement desensitization
  and reprocessing (EMDR),
  46, 236, 237

fantasy relaxation response
  technique, 245

fears
  anxiety is dangerous, 92, 141,
    142
  death and uncertainty, 145–
    47, 149
  embarrassment, 93
  judgment by others, 143, 144
  rejection, 93, 161
fight-or-flight response, 65, 71
flashbacks, 33
fortune-telling, 111
four-step approach to "what
  ifs," 130, 131–32

generalized anxiety disorder,
  231
genograms
  definition, 15, 16
  instructions for creating, 29
good day rule, 9
grief, 50
guidelines for practicing, 124

Herbert Benson's relaxation
  response technique, 244
holiday anxiety, 157
hyperventilation, 73, 74
hyperventilation. *See*
  diaphragmatic breathing, 89
hypervigilance, 4
hypnosis, 88

I messages, 182, 183, 187
indecision, 162
inferiority, 111, 112
insight-oriented psychology, 34
internalization, 64, 65, 79

Index

jealousy, 162, 164
journaling, 41, 80, 81, 137, 151, 152
judgment, trusting your, 158, 159

long-term recovery, 3, 5, 7
loss, 49, 50

magnification/minimization, 108, 109, 115
medication
  advanced symptom control and, 4
  basic symptom control and, 4
  cautions, 11, 12
  long-term recovery and, 5
  OCD and, 12
  sleep and, 44
message checklist, 194–96, 199, 200
mind reading, 110, 111, 142
minimization, 109, 115
mistakes, three-step problem-solving approach, 213

needs, see emotions, 52
negative anticipation, 64, 65
new car principle, 169
nocturnal panic attacks, 45
normal curve, 71
normalizing yourself, 68, 118, 142, 148

obsessive-compulsive disorder, 12, 229–30
overgeneralization, 104–8

panic attacks, 66, 226, 227
panic disorder with agoraphobia, 228
panic disorder without agoraphobia, 227
paper bag technique, 91, 98
perfectionism, 209–13, 217
personalization, 109, 110
phobias, 228, 229
posttraumatic stress disorder, 32–35, 146, 230
practice guidelines, 124
progressive desensitization, 120–38, 170
progressive relaxation, 88, 243
psychotherapy, 10, 233–38

redirection. *See* externalization, 96
relapses, 1–3
relaxation response, 242–45
relaxation response techniques, 42, 45, 88
responsibilities and rights, 184, 185
rights, 160, 161
rights and responsibilities, 184, 185
rituals, 230

sadness, 50
self-esteem, 201, 202, 216, 217
self-help groups, 11, 239–41
self-image. *See also* shame, 201–9
  trusting your judgment, 161
  viewing oneself and the world negatively, 38

Index

self-talk. *See also* coping self-statements; distorted thinking
  challenging irrational, 97, 112–17
  definition, 104
  journaling and, 151, 152
  negative common to anxiety, 140, 149
  sleeplessness and, 45
  two levels of challenging, 151, 152
setbacks, 176, 178–81, 186, 187, 219
shame, 148–50
should/must thinking, 105–8
situational nonassertiveness, 160
sleep, 42–46, 128
social phobia, 229
specific phobia, 228, 229
spirituality, 39, 53, 54, 192–94, 196, 198, 206–9
spouse/support person, 13, 14
stress
  decompression periods, 192
  developing a plan, 156
  diet and exercise, 191, 192, 196, 199
  exercise, 199
  guidelines for managing, 189–92, 196, 198
study partner, 11
substance-induced anxiety disorder, 232

suggestibility, 133–35
suicidal thoughts. *See* suggestibility, 133
summary card of basic symptom management skills, 102
summary sheets, 162–65, 168
  becoming friends with intimacy, 223, 224
  conflict is dangerous, 185, 186
  creating, 168
  excessive need for approval, 163–64
  going outside my "comfort zone," 174
  I must be strong, 177, 178
  I'm inferior to others, 203–5
  mistakes are terrible, 212–13
  perfection is impossible, 210–11
  things will always be the same, 173–74
  what makes me valuable?, 207, 208–9
support person/spouse, 13, 14

therapist, guidelines for selecting, 233–38
threat, 49, 50
three-step problem-solving approach to mistakes, 213
time tunnel, 31–41, 144
  definition, 35
  how to escape, 36

Index

unconscious associations, 56

"what if" thinking. *See* negative
    anticipation, 64
"what ifs," four-step approach,
    130, 131–32
white noise, 44

About the Author

Reneau Z. Peurifoy, M.A., M.F.C.C., has a private practice in Citrus Heights, a suburb of Sacramento, California. He first specialized in anxiety-related problems in 1981. Since 1988, he has conducted workshops at each National Conference on Anxiety Disorders presented by the Anxiety Disorders Association of America. He has spoken to groups and conducted training seminars on treating anxiety disorders nationwide.

Peurifoy also works with couples and individuals who have experienced early childhood trauma. He has designed and conducted educational programs on anxiety, anger, assertiveness, stress management, and other topics in a wide variety of settings. He has a special commitment to teaching effective parenting skills and has worked with more than two thousand parents in the various parenting classes he has taught.

Before deciding to go into counseling, Peurifoy spent five years as a teacher, two of which were spent in Japan teaching science at St. Joseph's College, an all-boys school in Yokohama. Peurifoy met his wife, Michiyo, in college. They were married in 1974 and together they have two children.

You've found the right self-help book.
Now, find the right treatment provider and support network.

It's time for you to contact the **Anxiety Disorders Association of America** for help, hope, and information to speed along your recovery. Ask us for information about our state-by-state lists of anxiety treatment providers, self-help groups, books, tapes, conferences . . . and more!

Receive a free issue of our 28-page newsletter full of treatment updates and medical research just for inquiring (please direct your inquiry to Department SHR).

For Fastest Service
Call (301) 231-9350 or
Fax (301) 231-7392
Ask for Department SHR

Or Write to:
Anxiety Disorders Association of America
Department SHR
6000 Executive Boulevard, Suite 513
Rockville, MD 20852